MW00632511

The Handbook for

Beginning Programmers

with Examples in JavaScript

Third Edition

Published by Maia L.L.C.
Idaho, U.S.A.

ISBN 978-0-9962463-1-6

The author and publisher of this book have used their best efforts in preparing this book, and the information contained in this book is believed to be reliable. These efforts include the development, research, and testing of the theories and computer programs in this book to determine their correctness. However, because of the possibility of human or mechanical error, the author and publisher make no warranty of any kind, expressed or implied, with regard to these programs or the documentation or information contained in this book. The author and publisher shall not be liable in any event for incidental or consequential damages in connection with or arising out of the furnishing, performance, or use of these programs.

Cover Photo

The cover photo is courtesy of Nicole Köhler. You can see more of her photographic work at pixabay.com.

Contents

Preface

Learning to program a computer is a frustrating task for many students. In my teaching experience I have found that much of this frustration comes because students are not shown enough programming examples. All of us learn by watching others, so why should learning to program a computer be any different? I wrote this book with minimal text but filled with computer programming examples and many hands on exercises to help beginning students learn computer programming more efficiently and thoroughly and with less frustration.

How to Use This Book

You can use this book as a tutorial or a reference. When using it as a tutorial, you will find it helpful to step through the example code line by line as if you were a computer. Doing this is sometimes called a **desk check** because you are checking the code on paper or "at your desk" instead of running it on a computer. To aid you in desk checking the example code, I have provided desk check locations throughout the book. Each desk check location includes a list of all the variables found in the corresponding example code and values for the input variables. To perform a desk check, step through the code as if you were the computer and change the value of each variable just as the computer would.

Conventions

Within the text of this book the following fonts and font styles are used.

- **Bolded text** is used to highlight an important term.
- *Italicized text* emphasizes certain words that might be missed by casual reading.
- <u>Underlined text</u> indicates a hyperlink to a website.
- `Fixed width font` is used to show computer code.
- Menu font shows the words that appear in a computer menu or on a computer button.

Chapters 5–12 include JavaScript code templates that use these fonts and symbols.

- `Fixed width font` is used for JavaScript keywords that you must type exactly as they are shown in the template.
- *Italicized text* is used for words that you should replace when you write code.
- Any part of a template that is written in gray text is optional.

For example within the following template, var is a JavaScript keyword, name2 and name3 are optional, and *name, name2,* and *name3* should be replaced by names that you choose.

```
var name, name2, name3…;
```

To aid in your learning, this book contains different types of learning tools such as

- places for you to take notes during class
- exercises that you will complete in class
- example code and tables to desk check that code
- review questions
- programming assignments

Locations within this book where you should write or do an exercise are marked in the margin with a pencil icon like this

Acknowledgments

I am grateful to Michael McLaughlin for our many discussions on pedagogy and student learning. I thank my wife for her support and proofreading of this book. I am also grateful to my students who have used this book and given me valuable suggestions, such as Adam Martin, one of my teaching assistants, who gave me valuable suggestions about the chapter on functions.

The quick response (QR) codes in this book were provided by kaywa at qrcode.kaywa.com The ISBN barcode was provided by Terry Burton at www.terryburton.co.uk/barcodewriter/generator

Review This Book

Please rate this book or write a review at www.amazon.com/dp/B00TEO4IVU. Your comments and suggestions help the author and publisher produce better books.

Chapter 1. Computer Hardware

Chapter Outcome

By the end of this chapter you will have a basic understanding of computer hardware so that you can begin to program computers.

Semiconductors

Many of the parts of a computer, including the CPU and main memory, are composed of millions or billions of microscopic semiconductors that are etched in silicon. The word semiconductor means these microscopic parts partially conduct or sometimes conduct electricity. There are many different types of semiconductors, and each type fulfills a specific purpose. Below is a list of common semiconductors and their purpose.

1. Capacitor – a semiconductor that temporarily stores electricity.

2. Diode – a semiconductor that allows electricity to flow in only one direction.

3. LED – acronym for light emitting diode; a diode that emits light when electricity is flowing through it.

4. Resistor – a semiconductor that resists the flow of electricity. A resistor is often used to protect other parts of a computer from surges in electricity.

a

b

c

d

e

5. Transistor – a semiconductor with two inputs and one output called the drain. A small current on the center wire of the transistor controls a larger current

Figure 1: Photographs of common semiconductors: a) capacitor, b) diode, c) light emitting diode, d) resistor, and e) transistor.

that flows on the two outer wires. A transistor can be used as an amplifier or an automated switch with the small electric current input controlling the larger input and output current.

6. Integrated circuit – a circuit composed of many (possibly billions) semiconductors etched on a small piece of silicon; sometimes called a computer chip.

Parts of a Computer

A modern computer is an electronic machine that is composed of two major parts: hardware and software. Computer hardware is the physical parts of a computer, such as the keyboard, mouse, CPU, hard drive, memory, monitor, and printer. An easy mnemonic to help you remember that hardware is the physical parts of a computer is that the physical parts are hard. If someone threw a piece of computer hardware at you, and it hit you, it would hurt. Of course each part of a computer has its own specific purpose. Here is a list of common computer hardware parts.

7. Power supply – an electric circuit that converts the electricity coming from an outlet in the wall, usually 115 volts, 60 Hertz alternating current (AC), into electricity that a computer can use, such as 3.3 volts direct current (DC).

8. Keyboard – an input device that allows a user to enter data into a computer by pressing keys.

9. Motherboard – the main circuit board to which the other parts of a computer are attached. Figure 2 shows a computer motherboard without a CPU, main memory, or other devices attached to it.

Figure 2: A computer motherboard.

10. Bus – the wires and integrated circuits that transfer data across the motherboard from one component to another.

11. BIOS – acronym for basic input and output system; usually flash memory installed on the motherboard that contains instructions the CPU executes when a computer is started.

12. CPU – acronym for central processing unit; a relatively large and expensive integrated circuit where most calculations are done within a computer.

13. Cache – a small amount of fast memory that temporarily stores data and instructions and is often located on the CPU. The cache contains a partial copy of the contents of main memory so that when the CPU needs data for a calculation, the CPU can get the data from the cache and does not have to wait for the data to come over a bus from main memory. Cache memory is **volatile** which means that when a computer is turned off or the electricity is removed, the contents of cache are lost.

Figure 3: The top and bottom of an Intel Core i7 processor. Picture is courtesy of Intel.

14. Main memory – integrated circuits that temporarily store data and instructions for the CPU; sometimes called random access memory (RAM). Main memory is volatile which means that when a computer is turned off, the contents of main memory are lost.

Figure 4: Four gigabytes of DDR random access memory. Photo is courtesy of newegg.com.

15. Hard drive – stores data semi-permanently usually on a spinning platter where microscopic spots have been magnetized to store data. A hard drive is **non-volatile** which means that when a computer is turned off, the contents of a hard drive are preserved. Figure 5 shows a hard drive with its cover removed to expose the platter and the head that moves above the platter and magnetizes microscopic spots on the platter.

Figure 5: A computer hard drive with its cover removed exposing the platter and the head that moves above the platter.

16. CD or DVD drive – reads and writes data semi-permanently to a disc using a laser. Compact discs (CD's) and digital versatile disks (DVD's) are non-volatile.

17. Jump, thumb, or flash drive – semi-permanent memory that can be read, written, and erased electrically. Jump drive, thumb drive, and flash drive are different names for the same type of memory device which stores data in flash memory. A solid state hard drive does not store data on a platter like a regular hard drive but instead stores data in flash memory. Flash memory is non-volatile.

18. Monitor – an output device that displays messages, images, etc. for a user to see.

Data Sizes

Each of the following terms is a measure of the amount of data that a computer can store or process.

19. bit – an abbreviation for binary digit. A binary digit is a column in a binary number where either 0 or 1 can appear

20. nibble – four bits joined together to form a binary number. The name nibble is an inside computing joke because a nibble is half of a byte.

21. byte – eight bits joined together to form a binary number.

22. kilobyte – a true kilobyte is 1024 (2^{10}) bytes and not just 1000 bytes.

23. megabyte – a true megabyte is 1,048,576 (2^{20}) bytes and not just 1,000,000 bytes.

24. gigabyte – 2^{30} bytes

25. terabyte – 2^{40} bytes

26. petabyte – 2^{50} bytes

27. exabyte – 2^{60} bytes

Clock Speeds

The clock within a CPU is a small electrical circuit that repeatedly produces an electric signal that pulses, meaning its voltage rises and falls similar to Figure 6. This electric signal pulses many times a second, and a single core on a CPU is designed to complete one instruction at the end of each pulse.

Figure 6: A graph of a pulsing electric signal showing three pulses or cycles.

Clock speed is measured in hertz. A single hertz is one cycle per second. A cycle is from any point in the pulse to where the pulse repeats. In other words, a single cycle starts immediately after the electric voltage falls, includes the voltage rising, and ends when the voltage falls again. Here are the terms used to measure clock speeds:

28. hertz – a unit of frequency equal to one cycle per second

29. megahertz – one million cycles per second

30. gigahertz – one billion cycles per second.

Many modern computers have clock speeds of 2.5 gigahertz or higher which means a single core on a CPU is designed to complete 2.5 billion instructions per second. Many CPU's have multiple cores. Each core performs calculations independently of the other cores. A quad core CPU with a clock speed of 2.5 gigahertz is designed to complete 10 billion (4 * 2.5 gigahertz) instructions per second. This is very fast.

Classes of Computers

Computers can be classified according to their size and primary purpose. Here are some common computer classes.

31. micro or personal computer – a computer designed to be used by only one person at a time, such as a smart phone, tablet computer, laptop computer, or desktop computer.

32. workstation – a powerful computer designed to be used by one person at a time and used to perform engineering, scientific, and medical tasks such as designing airplane parts or modeling biological processes.

33. mainframe – a very powerful computer designed to be used by many people at the same time to perform business or scientific tasks.

Categories of Software

Computer hardware is really just a bunch of metal that electricity can flow through in well-defined paths. Computer hardware will not do anything without some instructions. The instructions are written by a computer programmer and are called software. Computer software is simply a list of instructions that the computer hardware executes. Computer software can be classified according to its purpose.

34. Application – computer software that someone uses to accomplish a specific task, such as write a letter, balance an account, watch a movie, or play a game. Examples of applications include Microsoft Word and Excel, Google Chrome, and iTunes.

35. Operating system – computer software that manages the hardware and isolates the applications from the hardware so that the applications do not have to interact directly with the hardware. Examples of computer operating systems include Microsoft Windows, Mac OS X, VMS, Linux, HP-UX, and Solaris.

Character Data

Everything in a computer's memory is stored as a number or set of numbers. Everything. Pictures, songs, text, instructions, everything. Each text symbol is stored in the computer's memory as a number.

36. ASCII – an acronym for American Standard Code for Information Interchange; a coding system (essentially a table) with 128 rows that assigns a number to each English letter and common punctuation symbol. See asciitable.com

37. Unicode – a very large coding system that includes ASCII and assigns a number to symbols from many languages, such as English, Portuguese, Greek, Hebrew, Arabic, and Tagalog. See unicode.org

Execution Example

To help you understand how the parts of a computer work together, consider what happens when a user double clicks on a Microsoft Word document file (a file with a filename suffix of .docx).

1. The operating system commands the hard drive to copy the Microsoft Word Application (MS Word) into main memory.
2. The hard drive copies MS Word over a bus into main memory.
3. After MS Word is in main memory, the operating system executes MS Word and sends a command to MS Word telling it to open the document that the user double clicked on.
4. MS Word requests the operating system to read the document from the hard drive and to place it in main memory.
5. The operating system commands the hard drive to copy the document file into main memory.
6. The hard drive copies the document file over a bus into main memory.
7. For each character that is in the document
   a. MS Word reads the character's Unicode number from main memory and requests the operating system to draw that character in a window.
   b. The operating system, finds the Unicode number and its corresponding symbol in a table and draws the symbol.

Review Questions

1. Which of the following computer components primarily stores data? (Mark all that apply.)
   - a. power supply
   - b. keyboard
   - c. motherboard
   - d. bus
   - e. CPU
   - f. cache
   - g. main memory
   - h. hard drive
   - i. DVD drive
   - j. thumb drive
   - k. monitor

2. Match each of the following types of computer memory with the physical quantity that each manipulates to store data.
   - a. cache
   - b. main memory
   - c. flash memory
   - d. hard drive
   - e. DVD drive

   - i. light
   - ii. magnetization
   - iii. electric charge

3. Computer memory that is volatile must have electricity in order to store data. When electricity is turned off, volatile memory loses its data. Non-volatile memory stores data after electricity is turned off. Which of the following computer memory devices are volatile? (Mark all that apply.)
   - a. cache
   - b. main memory
   - c. flash memory
   - d. hard drive
   - e. DVD

4. Match each term to its corresponding size in bytes.
   - a. kilobyte
   - b. megabyte
   - c. gigabyte
   - d. terabyte
   - e. petabyte
   - f. exabyte

   - 1,125,899,906,842,624 bytes
   - 1024 bytes
   - 1,099,511,627,776 bytes
   - 1,073,741,824 bytes
   - 1,048,576 bytes
   - 1,152,921,504,606,846,976 bytes

5. Assume the average movie uses 3 gigabytes of space on a hard drive. Which of these is the smallest size that can store 200 average size movies?
   a. 500 megabytes
   b. 500 gigabytes
   c. 1 terabyte
   d. 1 petabyte

6. Consider a quad core CPU with a clock speed of 2.8 gigahertz. In theory, how many instructions per second is it able to complete?
   a. 2.8 million
   b. 2.8 billion
   c. 11.2 billion
   d. 20 billion

7. If you wanted to type a letter in Hebrew, which character coding system would your computer need to use to store your letter?
   a. ASCII
   b. Unicode

8. Which character coding system includes English letters? (Mark all that apply.)
   a. ASCII
   b. Unicode

1. Computer Hardware

Chapter 2. Algorithms and Computer Programs

Chapter Outcomes

By the end of this chapter you will:

- Read a description of a problem and write a defining table to help you better understand the problem.
- Develop an algorithm for a common task.
- Understand the basic operations that a computer can perform.
- Learn the three basic control structures: sequence, selection, and repetition, and what they cause a computer to do.

Defining Table

An **algorithm** is simply a list of steps to perform some task. A large computer program contains many algorithms. Before creating an algorithm to solve a problem, you must be sure that you understand the problem. If you don't, you will probably create an algorithm that solves the wrong problem. A **defining table** is a useful tool to help you better understand a problem before you develop an algorithm to solve it. A defining table has three sections: input, processing, and output. To create a defining table, simply draw a table with the three sections, and as you read and re-read the problem, put the parts of the problem into their correct section in the table.

Example 1

You work for a large construction company. Your boss has asked you to write a computer program that will read a list of window openings for a building and compute and output the total cost of all the windows. The window openings are entered in inches with the width first and the height second. The cost of a window is computed by multiplying the area of the window in square feet by $35.

Defining Table

Input	Processing	Output
A list of window openings For each window<ul><li>width in inches</li><li>height in inches</li></ul>	For each window<ul><li>compute area in sq ft</li><li>multiply area by $35</li><li>add cost of this window to the total cost</li></ul>	total cost of all windows

Example 2

You have been asked to write a program that will read from the keyboard the radius of a circle and will output to the monitor the diameter, circumference, and area of the circle.

Defining Table

Input	Processing	Output
radius	multiply radius by 2 $2\pi r$ πr^2	diameter circumference area

Algorithms

An **algorithm** is simply a list of steps to perform some task. A recipe is an example of an algorithm because the recipe lists the steps necessary for preparing some food. Here is a recipe from allrecipes.com for making chocolate chip cookies. Notice the directions which are what make a recipe similar to an algorithm.

Ingredients

- 1 cup butter, softened
- 1 cup white sugar
- 1 cup packed brown sugar
- 2 eggs
- 2 teaspoons vanilla extract
- 3 cups all-purpose flour
- 1 teaspoon baking soda
- 2 teaspoons hot water
- 1/2 teaspoon salt
- 2 cups semisweet chocolate chips
- 1 cup chopped walnuts

Directions

1. Preheat oven to 350 degrees F (175 degrees C).
2. Cream together the butter, white sugar, and brown sugar until smooth.
3. Beat in the eggs one at a time.
4. Stir in the vanilla.
5. Dissolve baking soda in hot water. Add to batter along with salt.
6. Stir in flour, chocolate chips, and nuts.
7. Drop by large spoonfuls onto ungreased pans.

8. Bake for about 10 minutes in the preheated oven, or until edges are nicely browned.

Here is a small algorithm for computing the average test score from a list of test scores. Notice that it is nothing more than the step by step process for performing the calculation. A large computer program contains many algorithms.

Example 3

1. Set *sum* to 0
2. Get the number of students
3. For each student
   a. Get the student's test score
   b. Add the student's score to the *sum*
4. Divide the *sum* by the number of students

Example 4

Write an algorithm to brush your teeth.

1. Get toothbrush wet
2. Put toothpaste on toothbrush
3. Apply toothbrush to teeth in a circular motion for two minutes
4. Spit toothpaste in sink
5. Rinse mouth + toothbrush

Within the algorithm that you wrote is the order of the steps important? Are there any steps that the order does not matter?

Computer Programs

A computer program is composed of data and instructions. The computer stores the data temporarily in its main memory. It also stores data more permanently in files on a hard drive, memory stick, or compact disk. The instructions in a computer program are like the steps in an algorithm. In a programming language like JavaScript, the instructions are called statements. A single **statement** is equivalent to a single step in an algorithm or a single sentence in a paragraph. The statements tell the computer what to do with the data.

Computer Operations

A computer has seven basic operations that it can perform, all of which we can use when writing algorithms in a computer program. A computer can:

1. Receive data (input)
   Input devices: keyboard, mouse, microphone, touch screen, temperature sensor, hard drive, flash drive, etc.

2. Write out data (output)
   Output devices: monitor, printer, speakers, lights, hard drive, flash drive, etc.

3. Assign a value to a variable or memory location

4. Perform arithmetic
   Operators: − (negation), * (multiplication), / (division), % (modulus), + (addition), − (subtraction)

5. Compare two values
   Relational operators: < (less than), <= (less than or equal), > (greater than), >= (greater than or equal), == (equal), != (not equal)

6. Repeat a group of actions

7. Call a function and return from that function

You will study and use each of these basic computer operations in later chapters of this text.

Control Structures

There are five different categories of **control structures** that you can use to control the order in which a computer executes the statements in your program. They are called control structures because they control the *order in which the computer executes statements* also called the **flow of execution**.

1. **sequence** – causes the computer to execute statements in the order they are written in a program, from top to bottom. This is the default control structure.

2. **selection** – causes the computer to select one group of statements to execute and another group or groups to skip. This is how a computer appears to make decisions.

3. **repetition** – causes the computer to repeat a group of statements.

4. **function call** and **return** – causes the computer to execute the statements in another function and return a result from the other function to the call point.

5. **try**, **catch**, and **throw** – are used to indicate an error occurred and to handle errors.

You will study, learn, and use the first four of these control structures in later chapters of this book. Sequence is the default control structure and is covered in all following chapters. Selection is taught in chapters 6 and 7. Repetition is taught in chapter 8 and again in chapter 10, and function call is taught in chapter 9.

Chapter Summary

- An algorithm is simply a list of steps to accomplish a task.
- Sometimes the order in which the steps are performed is very important.
- A defining table is a simple tool to help a programmer understand a problem before developing an algorithm to solve the problem. A defining table has three sections: input, processing, and output.
- A computer is capable of performing only a few basic operations:
  - receive input
  - display output
  - store data
  - perform arithmetic
  - compare values
  - repeat operations
  - call a function
- All high level tasks that a computer can do, such as edit photographs, play music, and search data are simply combinations of the basic operations.
- A computer program contains both data and instructions. In JavaScript, the instructions are called statements.
- The three basic control structures that a programmer uses to control the order in which a computer executes statements are sequence, selection, and repetition.

Review Questions

For each of the following problems write a defining table. Then write an algorithm with numbered steps to solve the problem. Then label each step with the name of the basic computer operation that the computer will use during that step.

1. Your company needs a program to compute the amount to charge customers for mowing their lawns for an entire season. An employee will type in the total area of the customer's lawn in square feet. Your company charges 10 cents per square foot to mow a lawn one time and will mow each lawn once a week for 15 weeks.

2. You have been asked to write a computer program that will output an employee's after tax pay. Your program will read from the keyboard the number of regular hours and overtime hours that the employee worked and the employee's regular hourly wage. The employee is paid a bonus of 1.5 times regular pay for each overtime hour worked. Tax is 15% of the employee's gross pay.

Chapter 3. HTML Basics

Hyper-text markup language (HTML) is a computer language that is used to write documents for the world wide web of information on the internet. There are several different versions of the HTML standard, with the most recent being XHTML 1.1 and HTML 5. This chapter will help you learn enough HTML 5 so that you can begin writing JavaScript code in your HTML documents.

Chapter Outcomes

By the end of this chapter you will be able to:

- Read and write simple HTML 5 documents.
- Use the online W3C Markup Validation Service to validate that an HTML 5 document is well-formed.
- Fix an HTML 5 document that does not validate.
- Use comments to add internal explanations to an HTML document.

Starting with HTML

To start writing HTML documents you must have a decent text editor, such as notepad++ (notepad-plus-plus.org/download),
TextWrangler (www.barebones.com/products/textwrangler), or
Sublime Text (www.sublimetext.com) and
a web browser, such as Google Chrome (google.com/chrome/browser),
installed on your computer. When you use your text editor to write an HTML document and then save the document, you must save the document with a suffix of .html

Document Type Declaration

All HTML 5 documents must begin with a document type declaration like this: `<!DOCTYPE HTML>`. It doesn't matter whether you write this declaration in upper or lower case or a mix of the two. This declaration tells the computer that what follows is an HTML 5 document. If you forget to put it at the top of an HTML document, your browser may recognize the document as an older version of HTML, and the document may be drawn incorrectly by your browser.

Comments

A comment in an HTML document is a note or documentation that a web designer writes for himself or other designers that will look at the HTML code. Comments are ignored by the computer. A comment in HTML begins with the symbols less than, exclamation mark, and two dashes, like this: `<!--` and ends with the symbols two dashes and greater than, like this: `-->`.

HTML Tags

An HTML **document** is composed of elements. An element is simply a part of an HTML document. Figure 7 shows an HTML element and all of its parts. Notice that an HTML **element** is composed of an opening tag, optional text, and a closing tag. A single **tag** begins with the less than symbol (<) and ends with the greater than symbol (>). For example `<div class="note" id="high">` or `</div>`. An opening tag contains a tag name and optionally some attributes. Each **attribute** is composed of a name and a value separated by an equal sign (=), such as `id="high"`. A closing tag has the same name as the opening tag, but the name is preceded by a slash character (/).

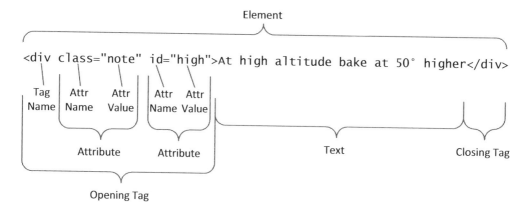

Figure 7: An HTML element and its parts. An element is composed of an opening tag, optional text, and a closing tag. An opening tag is composed of a tag name and optional attributes. An attribute is composed of a name and a value.

Sometimes the opening and closing tags are combined into one tag, such as:

```
<input type="text" id="futureValue" size="5" />
```

Notice the slash character (/) which is normally in the closing tag is at the end of the input tag above. The slash character appears at the end of this input tag because this tag is both an opening and closing tag combined together.

Hypertext Markup Language (HTML) is really just a list of tags that most web browsers understand. The following table lists most of the HTML tags that we will use in this class. A good reference that describes these tags in more detail is at w3schools.com.

HTML Tags

Opening and Closing Tags	Purpose
<!DOCTYPE HTML>	The document type declaration that must appear at the top of all HTML 5 documents. Technically, this declaration is not a tag, so it has no closing tag.
<!-- a comment here -->	A comment or notes seen only by the developers and not the users of a page. A comment is not a true tag, so it has no closing tag.
<html lang="en-us"> </html>	Begins and ends an HTML document; the first and last tags of an HTML document.
<head> </head>	Marks the start and end of the HTML document head. Every HTML document must have one head. The head contains information such as the title and author of the document and most JavaScript code.
<meta>	Provides information about a document, such as the author, descriptions, keywords, and the character encoding. (No closing tag.)
<title> </title>	Marks the title of a document. This tag should appear in the document head.
<script type="text/javascript"> </script>	Marks the start and end of JavaScript code. You can place a <script> tag in the head or body of an HTML document, but they are normally placed in the head.
<body> </body>	Marks the start and end of the document body. Every HTML document must have one body. The body contains the main information of a document that the user will see.

HTML Tags

Opening and Closing Tags	Purpose
`<div>` `</div>`	Marks the start and end of a division within an HTML document. The concept of division in HTML is very general and is simply a large, medium, or small section of a document.
`<h1>` `</h1>`	Marks the start and end of a level 1 heading. There are six different heading tags numbered from `<h1>` to `<h6>` with `<h1>` being the largest and `<h6>` being the smallest style of heading.
`<h2>` `</h2>`	Marks the start and end of a level 2 heading.
`<p>` `</p>`	Marks the limits of a paragraph.
` `	Forces the browser to insert a line break. (No closing tag.)
`<input type="text" id="years">`	Makes a text field (single row) where a user can enter data. (No closing tag.)
`<textarea>` `</textarea>`	Makes a text area (multiple rows) where a user can enter data.
`<button type="button" onclick="computeFV()">` `</button>`	Makes a button that a user can click.

Case Insensitive

HTML 5 is not case sensitive. This means that `<HTML>` and `<html>` and `<HtMl>` have the same meaning in HTML 5. However, the standard convention is to use all lower case for tags and attributes except for the DOCTYPE declaration which is all uppercase. Most developers use lower case letters for at least two reasons:

1. Lower case letters are easier to read because they vary in size more than upper case letters.
2. If an HTML 5 document is ever converted to XHTML, which requires lower case tags and attributes, the conversion will be easier.

Well Formed HTML

An HTML document should be well formed which means:

1. The document contains only the standard tags and attributes.
2. Most opening tags have a matching closing tag. The opening tags that don't require an closing tag are called **void tags** and include `<meta>` `<br>` and `<input>`.
3. Nested tags are ended before their enclosing tags are ended, for example:

```
<body>
<p>Oregano is an important <i>culinary</i> herb. It is used in Greek
and Italian dishes especially tomato based sauces, fried vegetables,
and grilled meats.</p>
</body>
```

You can check an HTML document to ensure that it is well formed by uploading it to the online validator at validator.w3.org

Required Tags

Every HTML 5 document must start with a `<!DOCTYPE>` declaration and an opening `<html>` tag. Every HTML 5 document must have a head section and a body section, and the head section should have a `<title>` tag and a `<meta>` tag that states the document's character encoding. In other words the skeleton of every HTML 5 document should look similar to this:

```
<!DOCTYPE HTML>
<html lang="en-us">
<head>
<meta charset="utf-8">
<title>Title</title>
</head>
<body>
</body>
</html>
```

Example HTML Document

Below is a well formed HTML 5 document that includes one comment and all the tags and text necessary for a web browser to draw the document. The document is shown drawn by the Firefox web browser in Figure 8.

Example 1

```
<!DOCTYPE HTML>
<html lang="en-us">
<head>

<!-- The following meta tag tells the browser that this document
     uses the 8-bit Unicode Transformation Format encoding. -->
<meta charset="utf-8">

<meta name="author" content="Rex Barzee">
<title>Horse Rentals</title>
</head>

<body>
<h1>Horse Rentals</h1>
<p>We rent horsies, big horsies, medium sized horsies, and little horsies
(big dogs really). Of course, this costs a great deal of money, and in order
for us to allow you to take the horsies anywhere, you must sign a lot of
paper work, about the same amount as if you were buying a house or being
admitted to a hospital (which might happen if you fall off one of our
horsies).</p>

<p>We rent horsy saddles and other leather and metal stuff. Just ask for
what you want, and we probably have it. These are mostly used to control the
horsies which they don't like. If you don't take great care when putting
these on the horsies, you might be admitted to the hospital as mentioned in
the above paragraph.</p>

<p>We also rent horsy trailers. These trailers require a truck the size of
Texas that drinks diesel in order to actually pull them. Of course, if you
don't have a truck that fits this description, we'll rent you one. See the
first paragraph again for our rental terms (big money).</p>
</body>
</html>
```

Handbook for Beginning Programmers

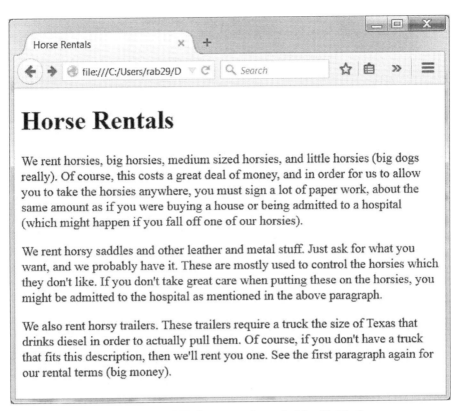

Figure 8: An HTML document drawn in Mozilla Firefox.

Example HTML Document with a Form

Below is a well formed HTML 5 document that includes all the tags and text necessary for a web browser to draw a document with two text fields, a text area, and two buttons. The document is shown drawn by the Firefox web browser in Figure 9.

Example 2

```
<!DOCTYPE HTML>
<html lang="en-us">
<head>

<!-- The following meta tag tells the browser that this document
     uses the 8-bit Unicode Transformation Format encoding. -->
<meta charset="utf-8">

<meta name="author" content="Rex Barzee">
<title>Send a Text Message</title>
</head>

<body>
<h1>Send a text message</h1>
<p>From (your 10-digit wireless phone number):
<input type="text" id="txtFrom" size="10">
</p>

<p>To (10-digit wireless phone number):
<input type="text" id="txtTo" size="10">
</p>

<p>Message:<br>
<textarea id="txaMessage" rows="8" cols="40">
</textarea>
</p>

<p><button type="button">Send</button>
<button type="button">Clear</button>
</p>
</body>
</html>
```

Figure 9: An HTML document that contains text fields and buttons drawn by Mozilla Firefox.

Common Mistakes

Forgetting the double quotes for an attribute

Incorrect
```
<div id="output></div>
```

Correct
```
<div id="output"></div>
```

Forgetting to end a tag

Incorrect
```
<div Idaho, with its volcanic
soils and cool nights, is ideal
for growing potatoes.</div>
```

Correct
```
<div>Idaho, with its volcanic
soils and cool nights, is ideal
for growing potatoes.</div>
```

Forgetting a closing tag

Incorrect
```
<b>really
```

Correct
```
<b>really</b>
```

Forgetting to save an HTML file with a suffix of .html

In order for a browser to detect that your file is an HTML file, you must save it with a suffix of .html

Chapter Summary

- Hyper-text markup language (HTML) is a computer language that is used to write documents.
- HTML 5 is the most recent version of HTML.
- An HTML 5 document must begin with a document type declaration and must contain a head and a body.
- HTML is composed of many tags. Each tag begins with a less than symbol (<) and ends with a greater than symbol (>).
- HTML tags usually come in pairs, an opening tag and a closing tag.
- Opening tags may contain attributes which are key/value pairs separated by the equal symbol (=).
- Opening tags that do not require a matching closing tag are called void tags.
- HTML tags should be properly nested.
- HTML is not case sensitive, so tags and attribute keys may be written in upper or lower case or any combination of upper and lower case.

Review Questions

1. What version of HTML will we use in this course?

2. Write the HTML 5 document type declaration as it should appear at the top of all HTML 5 documents. Include the surrounding less than (<) and greater than (>) symbols in your answer.

3. What is the first tag in an HTML 5 document? Include the surrounding less than (<) and greater than (>) symbols in your answer.

4. What are the two main sections that every HTML 5 document must have?

5. Inside which of the two main sections does the <title> tag belong?

6. What is the tag to begin the largest style of heading? Include the surrounding less than (<) and greater than (>) symbols in your answer.

7. What is the tag to begin a paragraph? Include the surrounding less than (<) and greater than (>) symbols in your answer.

8. What are the characters that begin an HTML comment?

Assignments

1. Create and validate a well formed HTML 5 document that tells a short version of your life story. The document must include at least one heading and two paragraphs.

2. Create and validate a well formed HTML 5 document that advertises a business that you own or would like to start. The document must include at least one heading and two paragraphs.

Chapter 4. JavaScript Basics

JavaScript was originally developed by Brendan Eich at Netscape under the name Mocha, later renamed LiveScript, and finally renamed JavaScript. JavaScript is most often used in web pages on the client side (web browser). Despite its name, JavaScript has very little in common with the Java programming language. The little that they have in common includes the syntax of the C programming language and some naming conventions and names, such as Date, Math, and String. You can find a good online tutorial for JavaScript w3schools.com and a good online reference for JavaScript at developer.mozilla.org

Chapter Outcomes

By the end of this chapter you will be able to:

- Read and write simple JavaScript programs embedded inside HTML documents.
- Write a JavaScript program that the computer runs when a user clicks a button.
- Write a JavaScript program that gets input from a popup window and sends output to a popup window.
- Write a JavaScript program that gets input from a text field and sends output to an HTML div.

Starting with JavaScript

Using your text editor, you can write JavaScript code in an HTML file. However, you must place the JavaScript code between opening and closing <script> tags as shown in example 1. Although it is possible to place <script> tags in the body of an HTML document, you should normally place <script> tags in the head of your HTML document. The HTML document from example 1 is shown drawn by the Firefox web browser in Figure 10.

Example 1

```
 1   <!DOCTYPE HTML>
 2   <html lang="en-us">
 3   <head>
 4   <meta charset="utf-8">
 5   <title>My First JavaScript Program</title>
 6   <script type="text/javascript">
 7   /* Defining Table
 8    * Input: No user input
 9    * Processing: None
10    * Output: The message "Water is delicious!"
11    */
12   function showMessage() {
13       // The next line of code causes the computer
14       // to open a popup window that contains the
15       // words "Water is delicious!"
16       window.alert("Water is delicious!");
17   }
18   </script>
19   </head>
20
21   <body>
22       <button type="button" onclick="showMessage()">Message</button>
23   </body>
24   </html>
```

Notice at line 22 in example 1 there are opening and closing button tags that create the button shown in Figure 10. Notice at line 22 that the button has an onclick attribute. When a user clicks this button, the computer executes the JavaScript code contained in the onclick attribute. The onclick code executes the showMessage function which begins at line 12 and ends at line 17. Within this function at line 16 is a command which causes the computer to open a popup window that contains the text "Water is delicious!" as shown in Figure 11.

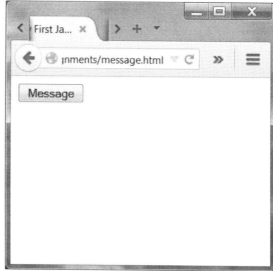

Figure 10: A simple HTML document with a single button drawn in Firefox.

To run the program in example 1, simply type all the code shown in example 1 (or copy and paste the code if you are reading this as an e-book) into a text editor. Don't type or copy the line numbers. Save the file with the suffix of .html, load the file in a browser, and click the Message button.

Running a Program

The computer runs or executes JavaScript code when certain events happen. These events include when an HTML document is loaded, when a user clicks a button, or even when a user moves the mouse. For example, the function in example 1 is executed when a user clicks the Message button.

Figure 11: A popup window that was opened by the Firefox browser because a user clicked the Message button.

Comments

A **comment** in a JavaScript program is a note or documentation that a programmer writes for himself or other programmers that will look at his code. Comments are ignored by the computer. There are two styles of comments in JavaScript: single line and multi-line. A single line comment begins with two forward slashes (//), and ends at the end of the line of text. A multi-line comment begins with a forward slash and an asterisk (/*), and ends with an asterisk and a forward slash (*/). When writing a multi-line comment, many programmers start each line with an asterisk to make the comment stand out from the other code. Both styles of comments are shown in example 1, multi-line at lines 7–11 and single line at lines 13–15.

Statements

A JavaScript program is composed of statements. A **statement** is a complete command within a program. Statements in JavaScript end with a semicolon (;). Notice in example 1 that the statement at line 16 ends with a semicolon. When writing a program, a programmer will often group statements together in a **block** by surrounding the statements with curly braces: { and }.

Case Sensitive

JavaScript is **case sensitive**, so if you want your JavaScript program to work, you must be careful to always type characters with the correct case. For example, to cause the computer to open a popup window, you must type `window.alert` not `Window.Alert`.

Declaring Variables

A **variable** is a location within the computer's memory to store data. When writing a computer program, a programmer declares variables so that the computer will reserve space in memory for the variables' contents. In JavaScript, we declare a variable by writing the keyword var and the variable's name. Here are several examples of declaring variables in JavaScript.

```
var price;
var numStudents;
var name;
```

String Concatenation

Within a JavaScript program a piece of text is called a **string** of text. In JavaScript you must surround all strings of text with quotes. It doesn't matter if you use single (') or double (") quotes, but you must be consistent. If you begin a string with a single quote then you must end it with a single quote. If you begin with double quotes, you must end with double quotes.

To create a large string of text from smaller strings of text you can use the **string concatenation** operator which is the plus symbol (+). For example:

```
var name = "Samantha";
var message = "Hello, " + name + ". How are you today?";
```

Popup Windows

A JavaScript program can get user input by opening a popup window where a user can type input. Example 2 contains an HTML document with a JavaScript program that

1. gets input from a user with a popup window
2. creates a greeting using string concatenation
3. displays that greeting to the user in another popup window

Example 2

```
1   <!DOCTYPE HTML>
2   <html lang="en-us">
3   <head>
4   <meta charset="utf-8">
5   <title>A Program to Say Hello</title>
6   <script type="text/javascript">
7   /* Defining Table
8    * Input: A person's name
9    * Processing: Create a greeting for that person
10   * Output: The greeting
11   */
12  function greetUser() {
13      // This line prompts the user to type in his name.
14      var name = window.prompt("Please enter your name");
15
16      // Create a personalized greeting for the user.
17      var greeting = "Hello " + name + ". I hope you are well today.";
18
19      // The next line causes the computer to display
20      // a greeting to the user in a popup window.
21      window.alert(greeting);
22  }
23  </script>
24  </head>
25
26  <body>
27      <button type="button" onclick="greetUser()">Hello</button>
28  </body>
29  </html>
```

The program in example 2 works like this:

1. A user clicks the Hello button.
2. The program executes the code in the `onclick` attribute of the Hello button.
3. The onclick attribute causes the computer to execute the code in the `greetUser` function.
4. Line 14 causes the computer to open a popup window which prompts the user to enter her name.
5. After the user enters her name, line 17 causes the computer creates a personalized greeting for the user.
6. Then line 21 causes the computer to display the greeting in another popup window.

Text Fields and Divisions

A JavaScript program can also get input from text fields within a document and send output to an HTML div. Recall from Chapter 3 that a div is simply a division or a part of an HTML document. Using text fields and divs for input and output is better than using popup windows because popup windows annoy most users. Example 3 and Figure 12 show a program that uses a text field for input and a div for output.

To get input from a text field, write an HTML document that contains a text field as shown on line 29 of example 3. Give the text field an id attribute. Each id within an HTML document must be unique. In other words, no other part of the HTML document is allowed to have the same id. The rules of HTML 5 require that the value of an id attribute cannot be empty and cannot contain spaces. In this book, we will use only English letters (A–Z and a–z) and Arabic digits (0–9) in the value of an id. For example:

```
<input type="text" id="salesInputBox">
<div id="output">
```

After adding a text field to your document, write a JavaScript function like the one that begins at line 12. Within that function write code that uses the built-in JavaScript function getElementById and the text field's id and value attributes to get the user's input as shown on line 15.

Example 3

```
1   <!DOCTYPE HTML>
2   <html lang="en-us">
3   <head>
4   <meta charset="utf-8">
5   <title>Applied Scripture</title>
6   <script type="text/javascript">
7   /* Defining Table
8    * Input: A person's name
9    * Processing: Create a verse of scripture for that person
10   * Output: The scripture
11   */
12  function applyScripture() {
13      // Get the user's name from the text field that has the id
14      // of "nameInputBox" and store it in a variable named name.
15      var name = document.getElementById('nameInputBox').value;
16
17      // Use string concatenation to create a verse
18      // of scripture personalized for the user.
19      var scripture = "I, " + name + ", having been born of" +
20          " goodly parents, therefore I was taught somewhat" +
21          " in all the learning of my father.";
```

```
22
23        // Display the scripture in the div that has the id "outputDiv".
24        document.getElementById('outputDiv').innerHTML = scripture;
25  }
26  </script>
27  </head>
28
29  <body>
30  Please enter your name: <input type="text" id="nameInputBox">
31  <button type="button" onclick="applyScripture()">Verse</button>
32  <div id="outputDiv"></div>
33  </body>
34  </html>
```

The program in example 3 works like this:

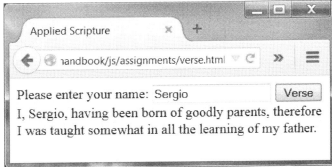

1. A user enters his name in the text field.
2. A user clicks the Verse button.
3. The program executes the code in the onclick attribute of the Verse button.

Figure 12: A program to create a personalized verse of scripture.

4. The onclick attribute causes the computer to execute the code in the applyScripture function.
5. Line 15 causes the computer to read the user's name from the text field.
6. Line 19 cause the computer to create a personalized verse of scripture for the user.
7. Then line 24 causes the computer to display the verse in a div for the user to see.

Reserved Words

The following is a list of all reserved words in JavaScript. You should not use any of these words as variable or function names in your JavaScript programs.

JavaScript Keywords

break	case	catch	continue
debugger	default	delete	do
else	false	finally	for
function	if	in	instanceof
let	new	null	return
switch	this	throw	true
try	typeof	undefined	var
while	with		

JavaScript Types

Array	Boolean	Date	Function
Math	Number	Object	RegExp
String			

JavaScript Objects

document	event	window

JavaScript Unused but Reserved Words

abstract	boolean	byte	char
class	const	double	enum
export	extends	final	float
goto	implements	import	int
interface	long	native	package
private	protected	public	short
static	super	synchronized	throws
transient	void	volatile	yield

Fixing a Program that Doesn't Work

After you have finished writing a JavaScript program, if it isn't working, do the following to find and fix the problems.

1. Make sure you saved your HTML file with the suffix .html
2. Validate your HTML file by uploading it to the online validator at validator.w3.org
3. Load your HTML document in a web browser and check the JavaScript console for errors. You can view the console in Google Chrome by pressing Shift-Ctrl-J (Windows and Linux) or Command-Option-J (Mac).
4. Click the button in your HTML document to execute your code and check the JavaScript console again for errors.
5. Use the JavaScript debugger that is built into your web browser to step through your code line by line and watch the values of the variables.

Common Mistakes

Misspelling onclick

Incorrect
```
<button type="button"
onlick="funcName()">
```

Correct
```
<button type="button"
onclick="funcName()">
```

Leaving the onclick attribute of a button empty

Incorrect
```
<button type="button"
onclick="">
```

Correct
```
<button type="button"
onclick="funcName()">
```

Forgetting the parentheses after the function name in the onclick attribute

Incorrect
```
<button type="button"
onclick="funcName">
```

Correct
```
<button type="button"
onclick="funcName()">
```

Chapter Summary

- Within an HTML document, JavaScript programs must be placed inside script tags.
- To cause a computer to execute a JavaScript program when a user clicks a button, the button must have an onclick attribute.
- A JavaScript program may get input from a popup window or from a text field.
- A JavaScript program may send output to a popup window or to an HTML div.
- To make a large string of text from smaller strings of text, use the string concatenation operator which is the plus symbol (+).

Review Questions

1. What is the HTML tag and attribute to put a text field in a document?

2. What is the HTML tag and attribute to put a div that can be used for output in a document?

3. What is the HTML attribute that a developer can use to uniquely identify each document element?

4. What is the HTML tag to put a button in a document?

5. What is the HTML attribute of a button that contains JavaScript code that will be executed when a user clicks on that button?

6. What is the HTML tag that begins a section of JavaScript code?

7. What is the JavaScript keyword to declare a variable?

8. What is the JavaScript code to find or get an HTML element based on the element's id attribute?

Programming Assignments

1. Type in the HTML and JavaScript code for example 2 in this chapter. Modify the code by changing the greeting that is displayed to the user. The changed greeting must include the user's name. Validate the code and load it in a web browser to run and test it.

2. Type in the HTML and JavaScript code for example 3 in this chapter. Modify the code by changing the scripture that is displayed to the user. The changed scripture must include the user's name. Validate the code and load it in a web browser to run and test it.

3. Create an HTML 5 document that you can use as a template for the programs you will write in this class in the future. This file should include the DOCTYPE, html, head, title, and body tags as well as a script tag and any other tags that you think would be helpful in a template for quickly creating HTML files that contain JavaScript programs.

4. Write an HTML 5 document which contains five text fields, a button, and a text area. Write and test a JavaScript program that reads user input from all five text fields and concatenates all the input into one address and outputs the address in the div as shown in Figure 13.

Figure 13: An HTML document and JavaScript program that accepts input from five text fields, combines the input into one address, and outputs the address to a div.

Chapter 5. Variables and Arithmetic

A computer program is composed of data and instructions. The data may be temporarily stored in the computer's memory, or it may be stored more permanently on the computer's hard drive or on a CD or tape. When data is in the computer's memory, it is stored inside variables. A **variable** has a name, type, value, and scope. The term variable comes from the fact that a variable's value can be changed or varied.

Chapter Outcomes

By the end of this chapter you will be able to:

- Declare a variable and assign a value to that variable.
- Write JavaScript code to copy the value from one variable to another variable.
- Write code to perform calculations and store the result in a variable.
- Use the increment and decrement operators in an arithmetic expression.
- Use the mathematical functions in the Math object.

Declaring a Variable

Before you can use a variable in a computer program, you must declare that variable which tells the computer to reserve space in main memory for that variable. To declare a variable in a JavaScript program, simply write the keyword var and the variable's name. A variable name must start with an uppercase or lowercase letter, the underscore (_), or the dollar sign ($). The rest of the name must be made of letters, digits (0–9), the underscore, or the dollar sign. A variable name cannot include spaces. It should be a meaningful name that curtly describes what the variable stores. A computer programmer uses a variable's **name** in a program as a representation of the variable's **value**. This is similar to how a variable is used in an algebraic equation.

Template

```
var name, name2, name3…;
```

Example 1

Declare three variables named x, balance, and interest.

```
var x;
var balance, interest;
```

Example 2

Declare two variables named roomNumber and occupants.

Variable Types

Each variable has a **type** so that the computer knows what kind of data can be stored in the variable and what operations the computer may perform on the variable. A variable's type is determined by the data that is stored in the variable. A variable in a JavaScript program may have any one of these types.

JavaScript Variable Types

Type	Purpose	Example
boolean	stores true or false	true
number	a number with or without a decimal point	74.3
string	a string of text	"San Diego"
function	a part of a program created using the keyword function	function () { return 27; }
object	an object such as an Array or Date	{name:"Sam", phone:"1788"}

Assigning a Value to a Variable

A programmer may assign a value to a variable at any point in a JavaScript program by using the assignment operator which is simply the equal symbol (=). The assignment operator works from right to left, copying the value that is on the right side of the equal symbol and storing it into the variable or location that is on the left side of the equal symbol.

Template

    name = value;

Example 3

Declare three variables named `price`, `discRate`, and `title`. Assign 12.95 and 0.25 to the first two variables and the text "A Poor Wayfaring Man of Grief" to the third variable.

```
var price, discRate;
var title;

price = 12.95;
discRate = 0.25;
title = "A Poor Wayfaring Man of Grief";
```

Notice that to store text in a variable, you must put quotes (either double or single) around the text, for example:

```
title = "A Poor Wayfaring Man of Grief";
```

In JavaScript the default value for all variables is undefined. If a programmer does not use the equal symbol (=) to assign a value to a variable, the value of that variable will be undefined, not 0, not null, but literally the value undefined. Obviously, undefined is not a number and cannot be successfully used as part of a calculation. To help ensure that all variables have a value other than undefined, the JavaScript language allows a programmer to assign a value to a variable when it is declared. This is sometimes called **initializing** a variable, and many programmers like it because it saves the programmer from writing an extra line of code.

Template

```
var name = value, name2 = value2, name3 = value3…;
```

Example 4

Declare a variable named `price` and assign the number 12.95 to it. Also declare a variable named `title` and assign the text "A Poor Wayfaring Man of Grief" to it.

```
var price = 12.95;
var title = "A Poor Wayfaring Man of Grief";
```

Example 5

Declare a variable named `occupants` and assign the value 3 to it.

Desk Checks

While reading the rest of this book, you will find it helpful to step through the example code line by line as if you were a computer. Doing this is sometimes called a **desk check** because you are checking the code on paper or "at your desk" instead of running it on a computer. To perform a desk check, draw a table that represents part of the computer's main memory. Step through the given code line by line as if you were the computer and change the value of each variable just as the computer would. For example if you were given the following code:

```
1   var x = 7;
2   var y = -3;
3   var a = x;
4   y = 4;
```

You would draw a table like this to represent part of the computer's main memory.

Desk Check

x	y	a
7	~~-3~~	7
	4	

Notice that the first line of the code changes the value of the variable x to 7, so in the table 7 is written underneath the heading "x". The second line of code changes y to -3, so -3 is written underneath "y". The third line of code copies the value of x into a, so 7 is written underneath "a". Finally, the last line of code changes the value of y to 4, so -3 is crossed through and 4 is written below "y".

Technically, writing one value beneath another as shown in the desk check table for y does not accurately model the way a computer stores a value in a variable. When a new value is assigned to a variable, the old value is replaced by the new value. To accurately model this in a desk check, we would erase the old value and replace it with the new value. However, to understand how code works, it is often helpful to see a history of the values that a variable has held over time, so when you complete the desk checks, you should cross through an old value and write a new value below the old one.

Sometimes example code requires input from the user or somewhere else. This input is given in the desk check table. For example, the code:

```
var y = x;
```

requires that the variable x already have a value. This value will be given in the desk check table:

Desk Check

x	y
15	

Swapping Values

If a program needs to exchange the value of one variable with another variable, or in other words swap their values, a common and easy way to do this is to use a temporary variable. The example code below uses a temporary variable named *swap* to exchange the values of two variables, *a* and *b*. Desk check this code. To perform a **desk check**, step through the example code line by line as if you were a computer and write the value for each variable in the empty boxes. A missing box is a hint that means there is no value for you to write in that spot.

Example 6

```
var swap = a;
a = b;
b = swap;
```

Desk Check

a	b	swap
8	−3	

Arithmetic Expressions

The word computer comes from the ability these machines have to compute values or in other words to perform arithmetic. A programmer tells the computer to perform arithmetic by writing arithmetic expressions in a program. An **arithmetic expression** is composed of **operands** (numbers and variables) and **operators** (addition, multiplication, etc.).

Arithmetic in JavaScript is written differently than it is written in algebra. For example in algebra, 3*x* means to multiply 3 times *x*. However, typing 3x in a JavaScript program will not cause the computer to multiply anything. Instead it will simply cause an error. If you want multiplication in JavaScript, you must use the multiplication operator (*) like this: 3 * x.

Arithmetic Operators

There are five basic arithmetic operations that a computer can perform: multiplication, division, modulus, addition, and subtraction. As explained earlier in this chapter, a computer can also assign a value to a variable. A programmer makes the computer perform these arithmetic operations by writing the corresponding operator (symbol) in a program. Here are the arithmetic operators available in JavaScript.

JavaScript Arithmetic Operators

Operator	Name	Algebraic Expression	JavaScript Expression
$-$	negation	$-r$	-r
*	multiplication	vt or $v \cdot t$ or $v \times t$	v * t
/	division	$x \div y$ or x / y	x / y
%	modulus	$r \bmod s$	r % s
+	addition	$p + q$	p + q
$-$	subtraction	$f - 3$	f - 3
=	assignment	$s = t$	s = t

Modulus

The **modulus** operator is sometimes called the remainder operator because it returns the remainder after division. However, its correct name is the modulus operator because it returns the **signed** remainder after division which means the remainder can be positive or negative. In JavaScript, the sign of a modulus result depends only on the sign of the dividend (operand on the left of the %).

Examples

$$
\begin{aligned}
7 \ \% \ 3 &= 1 \\
12 \ \% \ 3 &= 0 \\
-6 \ \% \ 4 &= -2 \\
6 \ \% \ -4 &= 2 \\
-6 \ \% \ -4 &= -2
\end{aligned}
$$

In addition to the basic arithmetic operators, most computer languages provide functions to compute exponentiation, square root, logarithms, sine, cosine, and others.

Operator Precedence

When an arithmetic expression includes two or more different operators, the result is often ambiguous. For example, what is the result of $7 - 3 * 2$? Is it 8 or 1? The answer depends on the order in which the arithmetic operations are done. Because of this ambiguity, programming languages include arithmetic operator **precedence** which determines which operator is evaluated first and which is evaluated last.

JavaScript Arithmetic Operator Precedence

Operator(s)	Name(s)	Precedence
( )	parentheses	Highest (evaluated first)
—	negation	
* / %	multiplication, division, modulus	
+ —	addition, subtraction	
=	assignment	Lowest (evaluated last)

When an expression includes two operators with the same precedence, the computer evaluates them from left to right. For example, in the arithmetic expression x / y * c, the computer will first divide x by y then multiply that result by c. When writing an arithmetic expression, if you need a lower precedence operator evaluated before a higher precedence one, you can add parentheses to change the evaluation order. The computer will always evaluate arithmetic that is inside parentheses first regardless of the operator precedence.

Example 7

Translate the algebraic equation $v = i\left(1 + \dfrac{a}{n}\right)\dfrac{y}{n}$ into JavaScript.

```
var v = i * (1 + a / n) * (y / n);
```

Example 8

Translate the algebraic equation $x = \dfrac{7}{2(r + 13)} - 3(a + bc)$ into JavaScript.

Celsius to Fahrenheit

The formula for converting a temperature in Celsius to Fahrenheit is $f = \frac{9}{5}c + 32$

Example 9 is a JavaScript program that uses this formula to convert a temperature entered by a user in Celsius to a temperature in Fahrenheit. Notice at line 14 of example 9 the program contains code to read the value that a user typed into a text field and to store that value in a variable named text. At line 17, the parseFloat function converts what the user typed from a string into a number. Line 17 is necessary because a computer always treats values typed by a user as if they were text. This is true no matter what the user types. If a user clicks in a text field and then presses the 5 key and then the 8 key, a human will look at the user input and think of it as the number 58, but a computer will treat it as the digit "5" followed by the digit "8". In other words, if you are writing a program to get user input and to perform calculations with that input, then your program must convert the user input from a string of text into a number before performing calculations with that number. Converting from text to a number is what the parseFloat function does as shown on line 17.

In JavaScript there are two functions to convert a string of text into a number: parseInt and parseFloat. parseInt converts a string to an integer. If a user enters text with digits after the decimal point, parseInt will convert only the digits before the decimal point and will ignore the digits after the decimal point. For example if a user enters "75.814", parseInt will convert that to the number 75. parseFloat converts a string to a number that may have digits after the decimal point. For example parseFloat will convert the string "75.814" to the number 75.814 or a close approximation to 75.814.

Example 9

```
1   <!DOCTYPE HTML>
2   <html lang="en-us">
3   <head>
4   <meta charset="utf-8">
5   <title>Convert Celsius to Fahrenheit</title>
6
7   <script type="text/javascript">
8   /* Input: a temperature in Celsius
9    * Processing: convert the temperature from Celsius to Fahrenheit
10   * Output: the temperature converted to Fahrenheit
11   */
12  function celsToFahr() {
13      // Read a Celsius temperature from the user.
14      var text = document.getElementById('celsiusInputBox').value;
15
16      // Convert what the user typed from text into a number.
17      var c = parseFloat(text);
18
19      // Convert the Celsius temperature into Fahrenheit.
20      var f = c * 9 / 5 + 32;
21
22      // Display the Fahrenheit temperature to the user.
23      document.getElementById('fahrenDiv').innerHTML = f;
24  }
25  </script>
26  </head>
27
28  <body>
29  Enter a temperature in Celsius: <input type="text" id="celsiusInputBox">
30  <button type="button" onclick="celsToFahr()">Convert</button>
31  <div id="fahrenDiv"></div>
32  </body>
33  </html>
```

Desk Check

text	c	c * 9	c * 9 / 5	f
"20"				

Fahrenheit to Celsius

The formula for converting a temperature in Fahrenheit to Celsius is $c = \dfrac{5}{9}(f - 32)$

In some programming languages, such as Java, C++, and C, this formula must be carefully written because in those languages 5 / 9 causes the computer to perform **integer division** which truncates the result by simply dropping the digits after the decimal point. Thus, in such languages 5 / 9 yields 0, and a programmer must write the code in a way to force the computer to perform floating point division instead of integer division. However, in JavaScript, the division operator always causes the computer to perform floating point division.

Example 10

```
<!DOCTYPE HTML>
<html lang="en-us">
<head>
<meta charset="utf-8">
<title>Convert Fahrenheit to Celsius</title>

<script type="text/javascript">
/* Input: a temperature in Fahrenheit
 * Processing: convert the temperature from Fahrenheit to Celsius
 * Output: the temperature converted to Celsius */
function fahrToCels() {
    // Read a Fahrenheit temperature from the user.
    var text = document.getElementById('fahrenInputBox').value;

    // Convert what the user typed from text into a number.
    var f = parseFloat(text);

    // Convert the Fahrenheit temperature into Celsius.
    var c = 5 / 9 * (f - 32);

    // Display the Celsius temperature to the user.
    document.getElementById('celsiusDiv').innerHTML = c;
}
</script>
</head>

<body>
Enter a temperature in Fahrenheit: <input type="text" id="fahrenInputBox">
<button type="button" onclick="fahrToCels()">Convert</button>
<div id="celsiusDiv"></div>
</body>
</html>
```

Desk Check

text	f	f − 32	5 / 9	c
"25"				

Handbook for Beginning Programmers

Assignment Operators

In addition to the arithmetic operators described above, JavaScript also has assignment operators that perform arithmetic. These operators are really shortcuts for performing arithmetic using the current value of a variable and then storing the result of the arithmetic back into that variable.

JavaScript Assignment Operators

Operator	Name	Example	Equivalent Expression
*=	multiplication assignment	x *= 5;	x = x * 5;
/=	division assignment	s /= t;	s = s / t;
%=	modulus assignment	w %= z;	w = w % z;
+=	addition assignment	x += y;	x = x + y;
-=	subtraction assignment	r -= t;	r = r - t;

For example, x += 2 is equivalent to x = x + 2. In other words the += operator is a combination of addition and assignment and is shortcut way of writing a command with both. Here are some interesting uses of the assignment operators and some equivalent statements. Understanding these examples will help you better understand the assignment operators.

Example 11

```
x += x;
// 1. retrieve the value in x
// 2. add the value in x to it
// 3. store the sum back in x
```

Equivalent Example

```
x *= 2;
// 1. retrieve the value in x
// 2. multiply that value by 2
// 3. store the sum back in x
```

Example 12

```
x -= x;
// 1. retrieve the value in x
// 2. subtract the value in x from it
// 3. store the difference back in x
```

Equivalent Example

```
x = 0;
// store 0 in x
```

Example 13

```
x *= -1;
// 1. retrieve the value in x
// 2. multiply that value by -1
// 3. store the product back in x
```

Equivalent Example

```
x = -x;
// change the sign of x
```

Imagine a program to compute the price of a pizza. The price of a large sized cheese pizza with no other toppings is $10.95. The price for each topping such as ham, peperoni, olives, and pineapple is $1.95. Here is a short example that uses the += operator to compute the price of a pizza.

Example 14

```
var price = 10.95;
var toppings = 3;
var perTopping = 1.45;
price += toppings * perTopping;
```

Desk Check

price	toppings	perTopping
~~10.95~~	3	1.45
15.30		

Now imagine a program to compute sales tax and the total amount that a customer owes. The next three examples show three different ways that a program could compute the total including sales tax that a customer owes.

Example 15

```
var subtotal = 175;
var tax = subtotal * 0.06;
var total = subtotal + tax;
```

Desk Check

subtotal	tax	total

Example 16

```
var total = 175;
var tax = total * 0.06;
total += tax;
```

Desk Check

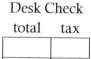

total	tax

Example 17

```
var total = 175;
total *= 1.06;
```

Desk Check

total

Increment and Decrement Operators

JavaScript includes two more shortcut operators called the increment and decrement operators. The increment operator (++) simply adds one to the value of a variable. The decrement operator (--) subtracts one from the value of a variable.

JavaScript Increment and Decrement Operators

Operator	Name	Example	Equivalent Expressions
++	pre-increment	++x;	x += 1; x = x + 1;
	post-increment	x++;	
--	pre-decrement	--t;	t -= 1; t = t - 1;
	post-decrement	t--;	

Both the increment and decrement operators can be written as a pre or post operator. If you write one of these operators before a variable name, such as ++x, then it is a pre-increment, meaning the computer will perform the increment *before* the rest of the arithmetic in the same statement. If you write one of the operators after a variable name, such as x++, then it is a post-increment, meaning the computer will perform the increment *after* the rest of the arithmetic in the same statement. However, if you use the increment or decrement operator in a statement all by itself, then it makes no difference whether you use the pre or post version. The next two examples show how pre and post-increment work when written inside a larger statement.

Example 18

```
var a = 4;
var b = ++a * 3 + 2;
```

Desk Check

a	b
4	17
5	

Example 19

```
var a = 4;
var b = a++ * 3 + 2;
```

Desk Check

a	b
4	14
5	

Notice in example 18, line 1 causes the computer to store the number 4 in the variable *a*. On line 2, because the increment operator is written as a pre-increment, the computer first adds 1 to the value of *a* and then performs the rest of the calculations on line 2 which results in 17 being stored in the variable *b*.

In example 19, line 1 causes the computer to store the number 4 in the variable *a*. On line 2, because the increment operator is written as a post-increment, the computer first performs the other calculations on line 2 which results in 14 being stored in *b* and then increments the value of *a* from 4 to 5. Notice in example 19 that incrementing *a* does not affect the value of *b* because the increment is a post-increment and the computer increments *a* after calculating the value of *b*.

When a new programmer first understands the post-increment operator, the most common question she asks is "Why? Why would anyone ever use the post-increment operator to change the value of a variable after the other calculations in the same statement are done?" The answer is "to prepare the incremented variable (*a* in examples 18 and 19) to be used later in the program."

When writing the increment or decrement operator, remember that it makes no difference whether you write the pre or post version of the operators if the operator is in a statement all by itself. For example:

```
a++;
```

Here are three more examples of using the increment and decrement operators.

Example 20

```
var x = 3;
var y = ++x * 2 + 5;
```

Desk Check

x	y

Example 21

```
var x = 3;
var y = x++ * 2 + 5;
```

Desk Check

x	y

Example 22

```
var q = 7;
var s = 2 + 18 / --q;
```

Desk Check

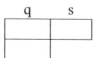

q	s

Handbook for Beginning Programmers

Operator Precedence Revisited

The following table shows the precedence for all the JavaScript arithmetic operators shown in this chapter.

JavaScript Arithmetic Operator Precedence

Operator(s)	Name(s)	Precedence
( )	parentheses	Highest (evaluated first)
−	negation	
++ --	increment, decrement	
* / %	multiplication, division, modulus	
+ −	addition, subtraction	
= += −= *= /= %=	assignment operators	Lowest (evaluated last)

Remember that the pre-increment is always executed before the rest of the arithmetic in the same statement, and the post-increment, even though it has a higher precedence, is always executed after the rest of the arithmetic in the same statement.

Math Object

The Math object is an object (see chapter 11) built into JavaScript that enables a program to perform more advanced mathematical computations. It contains the following mathematical constants and functions, all of which must be preceded by "Math." when you use them in a program.

Math Object Constants

Constant	Description	Algebraic Expression	Approximate Value
E	Euler's number	e	2.71828
LN2	Natural logarithm of 2	$\ln 2$	0.69315
LN10	Natural logarithm of 10	$\ln 10$	2.30259
LOG2E	Base-2 logarithm of Euler's number	$\log_2 e$	1.44270
LOG210	Base-10 logarithm of Euler's number	$\log_{10} e$	0.43429
PI	Ratio of a circle's circumference to its diameter	π	3.14159
SQRT1_2	Square root of ½	$\sqrt{½}$	0.70711
SQRT2	Square root of 2	$\sqrt{2}$	1.41421

Math Object Functions

Function	Description
abs(x)	absolute value of x
acos(x)	arccosine of x in radians
asin(x)	arcsine of x in radians
atan(x)	arctangent of x as a numeric value in the range $[-\pi/2, \pi/2]$ radians
atan2(y, x)	arctangent of the quotient of its arguments
ceil(x)	smallest integer that is larger than or equal to x
cos(x)	cosine of an angle x (x is in radians)
exp(x)	Euler's number raised to the power of x (e^x)
floor(x)	largest integer that is smaller than or equal to x
log(x)	natural logarithm of x ($\ln x$)
max(x, y, z…)	largest value of many numbers
min(x, y, z…)	smallest value of many numbers
pow(y, x)	y raised to the power of x (y^x)
random()	a pseudo random number in the range [0.0, 1.0)
round(x)	integer that is nearest x
sin(x)	sine of an angle x (x is in radians)

Math Object Functions

Function	Description
sqrt(x)	square root of x
tan(x)	tangent of an angle x (x is in radians)

Volume of a Cylinder

If we know the radius and length of a cylinder, we can compute the volume of that cylinder using the formula: $v = \pi r^2 h$ where v is the volume, r is the radius, and h is the length of the cylinder. This formula can be written in JavaScript as shown in the next example. Notice the use of the built-in JavaScript constant Math.PI.

Example 23

```
var v = Math.PI * r * r * h;
```

Desk Check

Figure 14: A cylinder with radius r and height h.

r	h	v
2.7	5	

Distance between Two Points

We can compute the distance between two points p_1 and p_2 in two-dimensional Cartesian space with the formula:

$$d = \sqrt{(x_2 - x_1)^2 + (y_2 - y_1)^2}$$

where d is the distance between the points, point p_1 has the coordinates (x_1, y_1), and point p_2 has the coordinates (x_2, y_2).

Example 24 contains a program that reads the x and y values for two points from a user and then computes and outputs the distance between those two points. Notice the code at lines 14–17 combines into a single line the code to read text from a text field and to convert that text into a number.

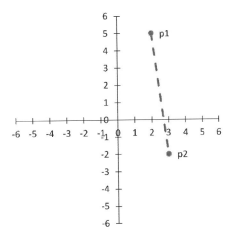

Figure 15: A plot of two points.

Example 24

```
1   <!DOCTYPE HTML>
2   <html lang="en-us">
3   <head>
4   <meta charset="utf-8">
5   <title>Distance</title>
6
7   <script type="text/javascript">
8   /* Input: x and y for two points: x1, y1, x2, y2
9    * Processing: Calculate the distance between the two points.
10   * Output: the distance
11   */
12  function distance() {
13      // Get the coordinates for two points from the user.
14      var x1 = parseFloat(document.getElementById('x1inputBox').value);
15      var y1 = parseFloat(document.getElementById('x2inputBox').value);
16      var x2 = parseFloat(document.getElementById('y1inputBox').value);
17      var y2 = parseFloat(document.getElementById('y2inputBox').value);
18
19      // Compute the distance between the two points.
20      var dx = x2 - x1;
21      var dy = y2 - y1;
22      var dist = Math.sqrt(dx * dx + dy * dy);
23
24      // Display the distance to the user.
25      document.getElementById('outputDiv').innerHTML = dist;
26  }
27  </script>
28  </head>
29
30  <body>
31  Please enter the x and y coordinates for two points:<br>
32  (x1, y1) <input type="text" id="x1inputBox" size="3">
33           <input type="text" id="y1inputBox" size="3"><br>
34  (x2, y2) <input type="text" id="x2inputBox" size="3">
35           <input type="text" id="y2inputBox" size="3"><br>
36  <button type="button" onclick="distance()">Distance</button>
37  <div id="outputDiv"></div>
38  </body>
39  </html>
```

Desk Check

x1	y1	x2	y2	dx	dy	dist
2	5	3	−2			

Round to Decimal Places

The built in JavaScript `Math` object has a function to round a real number to an integer. However, a programmer will occasionally need to write a program that rounds fractional numbers to a fixed number of places after the decimal point. For example, U.S. currency amounts are usually rounded to two decimal places (pennies). Here is code that uses the built in `Math.pow` and `Math.round` functions to round the value in a variable named *dist* to two decimal places.

Example 25

```
<script type="text/javascript">
/* Input: x and y for two points: x1, y1, x2, y2
 * Processing:
 *    1. Calculate the distance between the two points.
 *    2. Round the distance to two digits after the decimal.
 * Output: the rounded distance
 */
function distance() {
    // Get the coordinates for two points from the user.
    var x1 = parseFloat(document.getElementById('x1inputBox').value);
    var y1 = parseFloat(document.getElementById('x2inputBox').value);
    var x2 = parseFloat(document.getElementById('y1inputBox').value);
    var y2 = parseFloat(document.getElementById('y2inputBox').value);

    // Compute the distance between the two points.
    var dx = x2 - x1;
    var dy = y2 - y1;
    var dist = Math.sqrt(dx * dx + dy * dy);

    // Round the distance to two digits after the decimal.
    var digits = 2;
    var multiplier = Math.pow(10, digits);
    dist = Math.round(dist * multiplier) / multiplier;

    // Display the distance to the user.
    document.getElementById('outputDiv').innerHTML = dist;
}
</script>
```

Desk Check

x1	y1	x2	y2	dx	dy	dist	digits	multiplier
7	−2	4	6					

Common Mistakes

Forgetting to declare a variable

Incorrect
```
miles = 61;
```

Correct
```
var miles = 61;
```

Declaring the same variable twice

Incorrect
```
var total = 175;
var total *= 1.06;
```

Correct
```
var total = 175;
total *= 1.06;
```

Forgetting to type quotes around text

Incorrect
```
var speaker = Monson;
```

Correct
```
var speaker = 'Monson';
// or
var speaker = "Monson";
```

Forgetting to convert (parse) text to a number

Incorrect
```
var x = document.getElementById('num1').value;
var sum = x + 5;
```

Correct
```
var x = parseInt(document.getElementById('num1').value);
var sum = x + 5;
```

Using caret (^) for exponentiation

Incorrect
```
var g = (1 + r) ^ n;
```

Correct
```
var g = Math.pow(1 + r, n);
```

Using parentheses for multiplication

Incorrect
```
var z = 3(x + y);
```

Correct
```
var z = 3 * (x + y);
```

Chapter Summary

- Before using a variable in JavaScript, you must declare it. To declare a variable, write the keyword `var` followed by the variable's name.
- Use the assignment operator (=) to assign a value to a variable.
- Within a JavaScript program, use these operators: *, /, %, +, - to multiply, divide, compute the remainder after division, add, and subtract.
- To add one to the value of a variable, you can use the increment operator (++). You can use the decrement operator (--) to subtract one from the value of a variable.
- Each of the arithmetic operators has a precedence. It is important that you understand precedence when writing formulas in JavaScript.
- To program a computer to perform more advanced arithmetic such as exponentiation, square root, and rounding, you must use the functions in the `Math` object.

Review Questions

1. Declare two variables named `balance` and `rate`.

2. Declare a variable named `inventor` and assign the text "Franklin" to it.

3. Write a JavaScript statement to calculate the amount of energy released during a nuclear reaction. In other words, translate $E = mc^2$ into JavaScript. Assume that the variables m and c already exist and each holds a value. When writing your answer, be sure to declare E and use the variable names given in the equation above.

4. The semi-perimeter, s, of a triangle with side lengths a, b, and c is given by the formula:

$$s = \frac{a + b + c}{2}$$

Translate this formula into JavaScript. Assume that the variables a, b, and c already exist and each holds a value. When writing your answer, be sure to declare s and use the variable names given in the equation above.

5. Translate this formula into JavaScript:

$$r = 2k + \frac{6 - n}{3p^2}$$

Assume that the variables k, n, and p already exist and each holds a value. When writing your answer, be sure to declare r and use the variable names given in the equation above.

6. Rewrite the JavaScript statement: `z += x - 3 * y;`
   so that it doesn't use the += operator.

7. Rewrite the JavaScript statement: `b *= q - s;`
   so that it doesn't use the *= operator. Hint: pay close attention to operator precedence.

Programming Assignments

1. Write a defining table and a JavaScript program that asks a user for a volume in quarts and then converts that value into liters. Your program should correctly handle fractional numbers such as 7.54.

2. Write a defining table and a JavaScript program that asks a user for a distance in meters and then converts that value into miles, feet, and inches. Your program should correctly handle fractional numbers.

3. Write a defining table and a JavaScript program to compute and output the volume of a tin can. Hint: use the formula and JavaScript code given in this chapter to compute the volume of a cylinder. Your program should correctly handle fractional numbers.

4. Write a defining table and a JavaScript program to compute the mileage of a vehicle. Your program should allow the user to enter the beginning and ending odometer readings and the number of gallons of gasoline used and should output the mileage in miles per gallon. Your program should correctly handle fractional numbers.

5. When you exercise to strengthen your heart, you should maintain your heart rate within a range. To find that range, subtract your age from 220. This difference is your maximum heart rate per minute. Your heart simply will not beat faster than this maximum (220 – age). When exercising to strengthen your heart, you should keep your heart rate between 65% and 85% of your heart's maximum. Write a defining table and a JavaScript program that asks for a person's age and computes and outputs the slowest and fastest rates necessary to strengthen his heart.

6. Write a defining table and a JavaScript program to compute and output an employee's after tax pay. Your program will read from the keyboard the number of regular hours that an employee worked and that employee's wage, and then compute that employee's after tax pay. Tax is 15% of the employee's gross pay. Your program should correctly handle fractional numbers.

Chapter 6. Selection

In order for computer programs to be useful, a computer must be able to make decisions. The computer makes decisions by evaluating a condition and if the condition is true, selecting one set of statements to execute. If the condition evaluates to false, then the computer selects a different set of statements to execute. This decision making ability is known as **selection** because the computer is selecting either one group of statements or another group of statements to execute. A selection statement is also called an **if statement** because in most programming languages it starts with the keyword if.

Chapter Outcomes

By the end of this chapter you will be able to read and write:

- if statements with a single condition
- nested if statements
- a set of if…else if…else statements
- switch statements which can be used instead of a set of if…else if…else statements

Relational Operators

A selection statement always has a **condition** which is the test the computer uses to select one set of statements or the other. A condition always evaluates to either true or false. Any expression that evaluates to either true or false is called a **boolean** expression named after the British mathematician George Boole. There are six JavaScript **relational operators** which test the relation between two values and yield only true or false.

JavaScript Relational Operators

Operator	Name	Example
<	less than	if (i < 3)
>	greater than	if (x > y)
<=	less than or equal to	if (row <= end)
>=	greater than or equal to	if (age >= 8)
==	equal to	if (col == last)
!=	not equal to	if (col != last)

The relational operators are used inside the condition of selection statements. Shown below are the different forms of selection statements available in JavaScript.

if ...

Use when:

- A true choice exists and the false choice does not exist

Template

```
if (condition) {
    statements;
}
```

When the computer executes the condition, if the condition evaluates true, then the computer executes the statements inside the body of the if statement. Otherwise the computer skips the statements in the body of the if statement.

Example 1

```
if (balance > 500) {
    var interest = balance * 0.03;
    balance += interest;
}
document.getElementById('outputDiv').innerHTML = balance;
```

Figures 16 and 17 show the order in which the computer will execute the statements from example 1. Figure 16 shows that when *balance* is greater than 500, the computer will execute the statements inside the body of the if statement. Figure 17 shows that when *balance* is not greater than 500, the computer will skip the statements inside the body of the if statement.

Figure 16: When *balance* is greater than 500, the computer will execute the statements inside the body of the if statement.

Figure 17: When *balance* is not greater than 500, the computer will skip the statements inside the body of the if statement.

if ... else ...

Use when:
- A true and a false choice exists

Template

```
if (condition) {
    statements;
}
else {
    statements;
}
```

When the computer executes the condition, if the condition evaluates true, then the computer executes the statements inside the body of the if statement and skips the statements in the body of the else clause. Otherwise the computer skips the statements in the body of the if statement and executes the statements in the body of the else clause. The else clause is optional as shown in the previous section.

Example 2

```
var bonus;
if (sales <= 1000) {
    bonus = 20;
}
else {
    bonus = 100;
}
var salary = sales * 0.10 + bonus;
```

Figures 18 and 19 show the order in which the computer will execute the statements from example 2. Figure 18 shows that when *sales* is less than or equal to 1000, the computer will execute the statements inside the body of the if statement and skip the statements in the else. Figure 19 shows that when *sales* is greater than 1000, the computer will skip the statements inside the body of the if statement and execute the statements in the else.

```
var bonus;
if (sales <= 1000) {    (true)

        bonus = 20;
}
else {

    bonus = 100;
}
var salary = sales * 0.10 + bonus;
```

Desk Check

sales	bonus	salary
900	20	110

```
var bonus;
if (sales <= 1000) {    (false)

    bonus = 20;
}
else {

        bonus = 100;
}
var salary = sales * 0.10 + bonus;
```

Desk Check

sales	bonus	salary
1250	100	225

Figure 18: When *sales* is less than or equal to 1000, the computer will execute the statements inside the body of the `if` statement and skip the statements in the `else`.

Figure 19: When *sales* is greater than 1000, the computer will skip the statements inside the body of the `if` statement and execute the statements in the `else`.

if ... else if ... else ...

Use when:
- More than two choices exist
- Each choice is based on different variables or uses an operator other than equals (==)

Template

```
if (condition) {
    statements;
}
else if {
    statements;
}
...
else {
    statements;
}
```

When a group of if statements is connected using else, the computer evaluates the conditions one at a time until one of them evaluates true. The computer executes the statements inside the first if that evaluates true and skips all other statements. If none of the conditions evaluates true, the computer executes the statements in the last else clause only. The last else clause is optional as are all the else clauses.

Example 3

```
var discount;
if (cost < 100) {
    discount = 0.10;
}
else if (cost < 250) {
    discount = 0.15;
}
else if (cost < 400) {
    discount = 0.18;
}
else {
    discount = 0.20;
}
cost *= (1 - discount);
```

Figures 20, 21, and 22 show the order in which the computer will execute the statements from example 3. Figure 20 shows that when *cost* is less than 100, the computer will execute the statements inside the body of the first `if` statement and skip the statements in the `else` statements. Figure 21 shows that when *cost* is between 250 and 400, the computer will skip the statements inside the body of the first two `if` statements, execute the statements in the body of the third if statement, and then skip the last `else`. Figure 22 shows that when *cost* is greater than 400, the computer will skip the statements inside the bodies of the first three `if` statements and execute the code in the body of the last `else`.

Deck Check

cost	discount
~~70~~	0.10
63	

Figure 20: When *cost* is less than 100, the computer will execute the statements inside the body of the first `if` statement and skip the statements in the `else` statements.

Desk Check

cost	discount
~~300~~	0.18
246	

Figure 21: When *cost* is between 250 and 400, the computer will skip the statements inside the body of the first two `if` statements, execute the statements in the body of the third `if` statement, and then skip the last `else`.

Deck Check

cost	discount
~~480~~	0.20
384	

Figure 22: When *cost* is greater than 400, the computer will skip the statements inside the bodies of the first three `if` statements and execute the statements in the body of the last `else`.

Handbook for Beginning Programmers

switch

Use when:
- More than two choices exist
- Each choice is based on the same variable and uses equals (==)
- Comparison values are integer or string

Template

```
switch (variable) {
    case constValue1:   statements;   break;
    case constValue2:   statements;   break;
    ...
    default: statements;   break;
}
```

A switch statement functions like a group of connected if … else if … else statements that all test one variable for equality. When the computer executes a switch statement, it compares the value of the variable in the parentheses with each case one at a time. The computer skips statements for the cases that do not equal the value of the variable. It executes the statements after the first case that equals the value of the variable **and** continues executing statements in the switch until it encounters a break statement or the switch ends whichever happens first. If none of the cases equals the value of the variable, the computer skips the statements in all cases and executes the statements in the default case until it encounters a break or the switch ends. The default case is optional.

Example 4

```
var registerDate;
switch (classStanding) {
    case 'F':
        registerDate = "Nov 23";
        break;
    case 'S':
        registerDate = "Nov 17";
        break;
    case 'J':
        registerDate = "Nov 12";
        break;
    case 'N':
        registerDate = "Nov 6";
        break;
    default:
        registerDate = "none";
        window.alert("unknown class standing");
        break;
}
document.getElemenById('outputDiv').innerHTML = registerDate;
```

Desk Check

classStanding	registerDate
'F'	"Nov 23"

Desk Check

classStanding	registerDate
'J'	"Nov 12"

Desk Check

classStanding	registerDate
'Q'	"none"

Even Integers

The easiest way for a computer to determine if an integer is even is to divide the number by two, and if the remainder of this division is equal to zero, then the integer is even. The modulus operator performs integer division and returns the signed remainder of the division. The code example below uses the modulus operator to determine if an integer is even.

Example 5

```
<!DOCTYPE HTML>
<html lang="en-us">
<head>
<meta charset="utf-8">
<title>Is Even?</title>

<script type="text/javascript">
/* Input: An integer
 * Processing: Determine if the integer is even or odd
 * Output: A message that says the integer is even or odd
 */
function isEven() {
    // Get the user input from a text field and convert it to a number.
    var text = document.getElementById('integerInputBox').value;
    var value = parseInt(text);

    // Choose a message.
    var message;
    if ((value % 2) == 0) {
        message = value + " is an even integer";
    }
    else {
        message = value + " is an odd integer";
    }

    // Display the message to the user.
    document.getElementById('outputDiv').innerHTML = message;
}
</script>
</head>

<body>
Please enter an integer: <input type="text" id="integerInputBox">
<button type="button" onclick="isEven()">Is Even?</button>
<div id="outputDiv"></div>
</body>
</html>
```

Desk Check

text	value	value % 2	message
"8"			

Odd Integers

Because the result of the modulus operator is signed, when determining if an integer is even or odd the result of the modulus operator must always be compared to zero. Comparing the result to one will *not* work for negative, odd integers. Consider this JavaScript code and two corresponding desk checks.

Example 6

```
// Wrong! Doesn't work for negative odd integers!
if ((number % 2) == 1) {
    document.getElementById('outputDiv').innerHTML = number + ' is odd';
}
else {
    document.getElementById('outputDiv').innerHTML = number + ' is even';
}
```

Desk Check		
number	number % 2	output
5	1	"5 is odd"

Desk Check		
number	number % 2	output
−9	−1	"−9 is even"

Notice that comparing (value % 2) == 1 works fine for positive integers whether they are even or odd. However, as shown in the desk check above, it does *not* work for negative, odd integers. If you need to write code that takes action only if an integer is odd, the correct way to write the comparison is with the not equal relational operator (!=)

Example 7

```
// Correct check for odd integers
if ((value % 2) != 0) {
    document.getElementById('outputDiv').innerHTML = value + ' is odd';
}
```

Sometimes a programmer will use the bitwise And (&) operator to test if an integer is even as shown below. Such code works but is a bad solution for at least two reasons.

- It is not as straight forward as using the modulus operator.
- It depends on the computer using two's complement, binary representation for integers. (Admittedly, computers will continue to represent integers using two's complement for the foreseeable future.)

Example 8

```
// Correct, but poor check for even integers!
if ((value & 1) == 0) {
    document.getElementById('outputDiv').innerHTML = value + ' is even';
}
```

Many programmers write a test for even integers using the bitwise And operator because it may execute faster than a test using the modulus operator. However, the disadvantages of such code, almost never justify the very small, possible gain in execution speed, especially because most modern compilers will automatically optimize the compiled version of the statement using the modulus operator: if ((value % 2) == 0) to be the same as using the bitwise And operator: if ((value & 1) == 0)

Quadratic Formula

A quadratic equation of the form $y = ax^2 + bx + c$ has two solutions, also called roots, that may or may not be distinct and that may be real or complex. If you graph a quadratic equation, the roots are the locations where the equation crosses the x axis. Figure 23 contains the graph of three different quadratic equations. Notice that the first equation (on the left) crosses the x axis twice and therefore has two real roots. The second equation crosses or touches the x axis only once and therefore has only one distinct real root. The third equation doesn't cross the axis and so its two roots are **complex** meaning they contain the square root of -1. The square root of -1 doesn't exist, and mathematicians say it is **imaginary**.

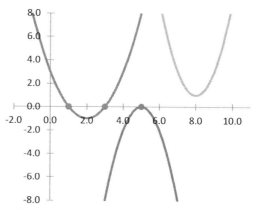

Figure 23: A graph of three quadratic equations.

The roots of a quadratic equation can be found using the quadratic formula:

$$x = \frac{-b \pm \sqrt{b^2 - 4ac}}{2a}$$

Handbook for Beginning Programmers

Here is JavaScript code for finding the real solutions of a quadratic equation if they exist. Notice the if statement that determines if the roots exist (are real) or don't exist (are complex).

Example 9

```
<!DOCTYPE HTML>
<html lang="en-us">
<head>
<meta charset="utf-8">
<title>Quadratic Formula</title>

<script type="text/javascript">
/* Input: Three coefificients from a quadratic equation.
 * Processing: If they exist, compute the root or roots of the equation
 * Output: The root or roots of the equation or
 *         "undefined" if they don't exist.
 */
function quadratic() {
    // Get three coefficients a, b, and c
    // for a quadratic equation from the user.
    var a = parseFloat(document.getElementById('aInputBox').value);
    var b = parseFloat(document.getElementById('bInputBox').value);
    var c = parseFloat(document.getElementById('cInputBox').value);

    // Compute the root or roots of the quadratic equation if they exist.
    var discr = b * b - 4 * a * c;
    var root1, root2;
    if (discr >= 0) {
        var sq = Math.sqrt(discr);
        root1 = (-b + sq) / (2 * a);
        root2 = (-b - sq) / (2 * a);
    }

    document.getElementById('outputDiv').innerHTML = root1 + ' ' + root2;
}
</script>
</head>

<body>
y = <input type="text" id="aInputBox" size="3"> x<sup>2</sup> +
    <input type="text" id="bInputBox" size="3"> x +
    <input type="text" id="cInputBox" size="3">
<button type="button" onclick="quadratic()">Compute Roots</button>
<div id="outputDiv"></div>
</body>
</html>
```

Desk Check

a	b	c	discr	sq	root1	root2
1	−4	3				

Nested If Statements

It is often useful to write one `if` statement inside another `if` statement or inside the `else` part of an `if` statement. Consider the problem to write a program that reads from the keyboard the total weekly sales for a sales person and then outputs the sales person's commission according to this table.

If the sales amount is greater than or equal to	And the sales amount is less than	Then the commission rate is
0	$300	0%
$300	$600	2.0%
$600	$1000	2.5%
$1000	∞	3.0%

This can be easily written using nested `if` statements as shown in the following code example. Notice the `if` statements nested inside the `else` statements.

Example 10

```
var sales = parseFloat(document.getElementById('salesInputBox').value);
var rate;
if (sales < 300) {
    rate = 0;
}
else {
    if (sales < 600) {
        rate = 0.02;
    }
    else {
        if (sales < 1000) {
            rate = 0.025;
        }
        else {
            rate = 0.03;
        }
    }
}
var commission = sales * rate;
var output = 'The employee earned ' + commission;
document.getElementById('outputDiv').innerHTML = output;
```

Desk Check

sales	rate	commission	output
850			

Although the previous example is correct, it can be written in a slightly shorter way by combining the else and if statements like this.

Example 11

```
var sales = parseFloat(document.getElementById('salesInputBox').value);
var rate;
if (sales < 300) {
    rate = 0;
}
else if (sales < 600) {
    rate = 0.02;
}
else if (sales < 1000) {
    rate = 0.025;
}
else {
    rate = 0.03;
}
var commission = sales * rate;
var output = 'The employee earned ' + commission;
document.getElementById('outputDiv').innerHTML = output;
```

Desk Check

sales	rate	commission	output
850			

As another example, consider a sports team that wants to provide discounted tickets to students and senior citizens and that wants to reward loyal fans that attend multiple games according to this table.

Age	Games Attended	Ticket Price
0 – 17	0 – 5	$8.00
0 – 17	6 – 10	$6.00
0 – 17	11 and up	$5.00
18 – 54	0 – 10	$10.00
18 – 54	11 and up	$8.00
55 and older	0 – 10	$8.00
55 and older	11 and up	$6.00

This could also be solved using nested if statements as shown in the next example.

Example 12

```
<!DOCTYPE HTML>
<html lang="en-us">
<head>
<meta charset="utf-8">
<title>Ticket Price</title>
<script type="text/javascript">
/* Input: A person's age and the number of games that person has attended
 * Processing: Determine the price to charge a person for a ticket to a game
 * Output: The ticket price */
function ticketPrice() {
    var age = parseInt(document.getElementById('ageBox').value);
    var gamesAttended = parseInt(document.getElementById('gamesBox').value);
    var price;
    if (age < 18) {
        if (gamesAttended < 6)
            price = 8.0;
        else if (gamesAttended < 11)
            price = 6.0;
        else
            price = 5.0;
    }
    else if (age < 55) {
        if (gamesAttended < 11)
            price = 10.0;
        else
            price = 8.0;
    }
    else {
        if (gamesAttended < 11)
            price = 8.0;
        else
            price = 6.0;
    }

    document.getElementById('priceDiv').innerHTML = price;
}
</script>
</head>

<body>
Age: <input type="text" id="ageBox" size="3"><br>
Number of games attended: <input type="text" id="gamesBox" size="3"><br>
<button type="button" onclick="ticketPrice()">Ticket Price</button>
<div id="priceDiv"></div>
</body>
</html>
```

Desk Check

age	gamesAttended	price
38	6	

Sometimes nested `if` statements can be a little tricky as shown in the following example which has two `if` statements but only one `else` clause. According to the rules of JavaScript, an `else` statement is paired with only one `if` statement. This means that in the example code below, if the first condition (x < 2) is true and the second condition (y > 8) is false, the computer will not change message to either "Hello" or "Goodbye". In that situation the computer will display "Wave".

Example 13

```
var message = 'Wave';
if (x < 2) {
    if (y > 8) {
        message = 'Hello';
    }
}
else {
    message = 'Goodbye';
}
document.getElementById('outputDiv').innerHTML = message;
```

Desk Check

x	y	message
1	5	

Common Mistakes

Forgetting parentheses around the condition

Incorrect
```
if x < 7 {
}
```

Correct
```
if (x < 7) {
}
```

Using assignment instead of comparison

Incorrect
```
if (age = 18) {
}
```

Correct
```
if (age == 18) {
}
```

Placing a semicolon at the end of an if statement

Incorrect
```
if (growth > 500); {
}
```

Correct
```
if (growth > 500) {
}
```

Placing a semicolon at the end of an else clause

Incorrect
```
if (growth > 500) {
}
else; {
}
```

Correct
```
if (growth > 500) {
}
else {
}
```

Forgetting braces when there is more than one statement inside an `if` statement

Incorrect
```
if (bal > 500)
    var intr = bal * 0.03;
    bal += intr;
```

Correct
```
if (bal > 500) {
    var intr = bal * 0.03;
    bal += intr;
}
```

Adding a condition to an else clause

Incorrect
```
if (gender == 'F') {
}
else (gender == 'M') {
}
```

Correct
```
if (gender == 'F') {
}
else {
}
```

Chapter Summary

- Selection is a control structure that allows the computer to execute one group of statements and skip another group of statements.
- An `if` statement is a selection statement that begins with the JavaScript keyword `if`.
- An `if` statement must have a condition in parentheses. The parentheses contain code to compare two values.
- There are six comparison operators in JavaScript: equal to (==), not equal to (!=), less than (<), less than or equal to (<=), greater than (>), greater than or equal to (>=).
- A `switch` statement is a selection statement that begins with the JavaScript keyword switch and can be used instead of a long set of `if` … `else if` … `else` statements.

Review Questions

1. Write an `if` statement to check if the value in the variable x is less than the value in the variable y.

2. Write an `if` statement that displays "go south" if the value in the variable temperature is less than 32, and displays "enjoy" otherwise.

Programming Assignments

1. Write a defining table and then a program that computes and outputs the absolute difference between two numbers entered by a user. In other words, your program should always show the difference as a positive number. Examples:

Numbers		Output
6	8	2
8	6	2
−3	5	8
5	−3	8
−7	−4	3
−4	−7	3

2. Write a defining table and a program that helps a user choose the correct foot wear for the day's weather. The following table shows the weather types the user may enter and what your program should output.

Weather	Foot Wear
hot	sandals
rain	galoshes
snow	boots

If the user enters any other weather type, your program should output "shoes".

3. A bank will not loan money to a home buyer unless the home buyer pays for part of the house at the time of purchase. This initial payment is called a down payment and is based on the cost of the home. The Bank of Ririe calculates down payments according to this schedule:

Cost of House			Down Payment
$0	–	$49,999.99	5% * cost
$50,000	–	$99,999.99	$2,000 + 10% * (cost − $50,000)
$100,000	–	$199,999.99	$7,500 + 20% * (cost − $100,000)
$200,000	–	∞	$27,500 + 25% * (cost − $200,000)

For example a house that costs $126,900 would have a down payment of 7,500 + 20% * (126,900 − 100,000) = $12,880. Write a defining table and a program that gets the cost of a house from a user and calculates and outputs the down payment based on the Bank of Ririe's schedule.

4. Write a defining table and a program to quiz a child on simple arithmetic. The program should allow a child to enter two numbers and an arithmetic operator (+, −, *, or /) and the child's answer to the problem. The program should compute the correct answer and compare it to the child's answer and output "Correct! Good job." or "Incorrect. Try again!" The user interface for your program should look similar to Figure 24.

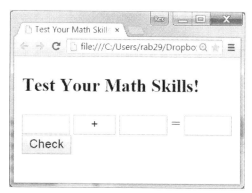

Figure 24: The user interface for a program to quiz children on arithmetic.

5. Roman numerals are still used today to display a year on the cornerstone of buildings. Write a defining table and then a program to convert a four digit decimal number into Roman numerals. The Roman number system has the digits

Roman	Arabic
I	1
V	5
X	10
L	50
C	100
D	500
M	1000

The rules for writing Roman numerals are

a. Thousands, hundreds, tens, and ones are expressed separately.
b. The numbers 1 to 9 are I, II, III, IV, V, VI, VII, VIII, IX
c. Tens are written the same way, except X, L, and C are used: X, XX, XXX, XL, L, LX, LXX, LXXX, XC
d. Hundreds are written the same way, except C, D, and M are used: C, CC, CCC, CD, D, DC, DCC, DCCC, CM
e. Thousands can be no larger than 3000 and are M, MM, MMM

As an example, 1987 is MCMLXXXVII (1000 = M, 900 = CM, 80 = LXXX, and 7 = VII).

Chapter 7. Logic

When writing a condition in an `if` statement, we often want the computer to evaluate more than one comparison. For example, we may want the computer to check if a person is male and older than forty. To combine more than one comparison within an `if` statement we use the logical operators.

Chapter Outcomes

By the end of this chapter you will be able to:

- Read and write `if` statements with multiple comparisons in the condition.
- Understand the logical operators: Not (!), And (&&), Inclusive Or (| |), and Exclusive Or (^).
- Use the logical operators to refine online searches.
- Write truth tables to help you evaluate and rewrite logical expressions.

Logical Operators

To combine two or more comparisons in the condition of a single `if` statement, we use the logical operators, also called the boolean operators. The following table describes the four JavaScript logical operators.

JavaScript Logical Operators

Operator	Name	Description
!	Not	Unary operator that reverses or switches a false value to true and a true value to false.
&&	And	Binary operator that combines two conditions, and the combined condition is true, if and only if both conditions are true, otherwise the combined condition is false.
| |	Inclusive Or (Or)	Binary operator that combines two conditions, and the combined condition is true, if either or both conditions are true, otherwise the combined condition is false.
^	Exclusive Or (Xor)	Binary operator that combines two conditions, and the combined condition is true, if and only if one condition is true and the other is false, otherwise the combined condition is false.

Notice that Inclusive Or is often abbreviated as Or, and Exclusive Or is often abbreviated as Xor. Notice also that Not (!) is a unary operator which means it operates on only one value, unlike And (&&), Or (||), and Xor (^) which are binary operators. Because Not is a unary operator, it has a higher precedence than the other logical operators.

Template

```
if (condition1 OPERATOR condition2) {
    statements;
}
```

Example 1

```
if (balance > 0 && daysSincePayment > 30) {
    balance += latePenalty;
}

if (sqft < 1500 || height > 30) {
    approved = false;
}
```

Disneyland Autopia

According to the Disneyland website, guests wishing to drive a car on the Autopia must meet one of the following height requirements:

- 54 inches (137 cm) or taller to drive alone
- 32 inches (81 cm) or taller and accompanied by a passenger 54 inches or taller

Here is a JavaScript program that accepts the height of a driver and an optional passenger and uses the logical operators || and && to determine if they may ride the Autopia. Notice the use of parentheses in the if statement to ensure the logic is correct. The program outputs either "Enjoy the ride!" or "Sorry, to drive a car on the Autopia you must be at least 54 inches tall or at least 32 inches tall and accompanied by a passenger who is at least 54 inches tall."

Example 2

```
<!DOCTYPE HTML>
<html lang="en-us">
<head>
<meta charset="utf-8">
<title>Are you tall enough to drive on the Autopia?</title>

<script type="text/javascript">
/* Input: the height of a driver and an optional passenger
 * Processing: Determine if a driver and
 *     optional passenger may ride the Autopia
 * Output: "Enjoy the ride!" or
 *     "Sorry, to drive a car on the Autopia you must be
 *     at least 54 inches tall or at least 32 inches tall and
 *     accompanied by a passenger who is at least 54 inches tall."
 */
function checkHeight() {
    var driver = parseInt(document.getElementById('driverBox').value);
    var passenger = parseInt(document.getElementById('passengerBox').value);

    var message;
    if (driver >= 54 || (driver >= 32 && passenger >= 54)) {
        message = 'Enjoy the ride!';
    }
    else {
        message = 'Sorry, to drive a car on the Autopia you must be
            at least 54 inches tall or at least 32 inches tall and
            accompanied by a passenger who is at least 54 inches tall.';
    }

    document.getElementById('outputDiv').innerHTML = message;
}
</script>
</head>

<body>
<h1>Are you tall enough to drive on the Autopia?</h1>
Driver's height in inches:
    <input type="text" id="driverBox" size="3"><br>
Passenger's height in inches:
    <input type="text" id="passengerBox" size="3" value="0"><br>
<button type="button" onclick="checkHeight()">Check Height</button>
<div id="outputDiv"></div>
</body>
</html>
```

Desk Check

driver	passenger	message
48	56	

Advanced Word Search

The logical operators &&, ||, and ! can be used when searching for documents on your computer or on the internet. At google and other search engines, this is often known as advanced search and can be very powerful. Learning to use advanced search will make you more efficient when searching for information and will help you better understand boolean logic.

Example 3

Imagine you are trying to find the web page for every Madison County in the United States except Idaho. To find these web pages, you might think of a boolean logic query such as

```
madison && (county || parish) && !idaho
```

meaning look for all documents that include "Madison" and either "County" or "Parish" (because Louisiana has parishes and not counties) but exclude "Idaho". Using the advanced search form at google, we enter madison, county, parish, and idaho in the correct text boxes as shown in Figure 25. Notice in the top most text box of Figure 25 that the google advanced search form wrote the search query as I entered the words in the other text boxes. From this we learn that the google advanced query that corresponds to our boolean logic query is

```
madison county OR parish -idaho
```

The google advanced query doesn't require the And (&&) operator or parentheses. If there is no operator between two words, the google search engine assumes the user meant And. Also, the Or operator has a higher precedence than And, so the parentheses are unnecessary in our particular search.

Figure 25: The advanced search page at google.

Example 4

Look on the internet to find a small flatbed trailer to purchase in southeast Idaho. craigslist.org is a good place to look for advertisements selling a trailer. Unfortunately, at craigslist there isn't a single category for trailers. Instead trailers are listed in the bikes, cars+trucks, farm+garden, motorcycles, and rvs categories. It would take far too long to look in all of these categories. So, use google to do the search and restrict the search to craigslist and cast Idaho.

1. At craigslist.org, click "idaho" then "east idaho" and notice the domain for eastern Idaho is eastidaho.craigslist.org.
2. At google use advanced search with the following criteria:

```
flatbed trailer -gooseneck site:eastidaho.craigslist.org
```

which will cause google to search for advertisements posted to craigslist to sell a flatbed, non-gooseneck trailer in east Idaho. To better understand this google search criteria, notice that it can be rewritten to use JavaScript boolean logic operators like this:

```
flatbed && trailer && !gooseneck && site==eastidaho.craigslist.org
```

Logical Equivalences

A logical expression can be written in many different ways that resolve to the same result. Two different logical expressions that resolve to the same result are said to be **equivalent** which is shown with a double ended arrow (⇔). Two such expressions are not the same and are not equal but are equivalent. Here is a list of logical expressions with an equivalent expression for each.

1. double negation: Not Not a ⇔ a
2. commutative laws:
    a. a Or b ⇔ b Or a
    b. a And b ⇔ b And a
3. associative laws
    a. (a Or b) Or c ⇔ a Or (b Or c)
    b. (a And b) And c ⇔ a And (b And c)
4. distributive laws
    a. a Or (b And c) ⇔ (a Or b) And (a Or c)
    b. a And (b Or c) ⇔ (a And b) Or (a And c)
5. idempotent laws
    a. a Or a ⇔ a
    b. a And a ⇔ a
6. identity laws
    a. a Or false ⇔ a
    b. a Or true ⇔ true
    c. a And false ⇔ false
    d. a And true ⇔ a
7. negation laws
    a. a Or Not a ⇔ true
    b. a And Not a ⇔ false
8. absorption laws
    a. a Or (a And b) ⇔ a
    b. a And (a Or b) ⇔ a
9. De Morgan's laws
    a. Not (a Or b) ⇔ Not a And Not b
    b. Not (a And b) ⇔ Not a Or Not b
    c. a Or b ⇔ Not (Not a And Not b)
    d. a And b ⇔ Not (Not a Or Not b)

Handbook for Beginning Programmers

Truth Tables

Truth tables can help us to write simpler boolean expressions and allow us to prove certain propositions about boolean expressions. We create a truth table by considering two or more conditions. These can be any conditions, for example "if (gpa > 3.5)" or "if (balance > 100)". We label these conditions *a*, *b*, *c*, etc. Then in the columns beneath the named conditions (*a*, *b*, *c*, etc.), we write all possible combinations of the values of these conditions. For example, if a boolean expression includes two conditions, *a* and *b*, then

1. both the conditions may be false;
2. *a* may be false and *b* true;
3. *b* may be false and *a* true; or
4. both may be true.

These four combinations are shown in the truth tables below.

Example 5

Given any two conditions *a* and *b*, show Not a, Not b, a And b, a Or b, a Xor b

a	b	!a	!b	a && b	a || b	a ^ b
False	False	True	True	False	False	False
False	True	True	False	False	True	True
True	False	False	True	False	True	True
True	True	False	False	True	True	False

Example 6

Given any two conditions *a* and *b*, show the result of (a Or b) And Not a
To solve this problem:

1.   We draw a truth table with a row for the headings and four rows for boolean values.
2.   In columns *1* and *2* we write the headings **a** and **b** and all possible combinations of true and false.
3.   In columns *3*, *4*, and *5* we translate the logical expression: (a Or b) And Not a into JavaScript operators: (a || b) && !a
4.   We write the result of (a || b) in column *3*. We write column *3* before columns *4* and *5* because a || b is inside parentheses.
5.   We write the result of !a in column *4*. We write column *4* before column *5* because Not is a unary operator and has a higher precedence than And.
6.   Finally, in column *5* we combine the results of columns *3* and *4* using &&. Column *5* is the result of (a Or b) And Not a.

1	*2*	*3*	*5*	*4*
a	**b**	**(a || b)**	**&&**	**!a**
False	False	False	False	True
False	True	True	True	True
True	False	True	False	False
True	True	True	False	False

Example 7

Given any two conditions *a* and *b*, prove that Not (a Or b) ⇔ Not a And Not b
To solve this problem:

1.   We draw a truth table with a row for the headings and four rows for boolean values.
2.   In columns *1* and *2* we write the headings **a** and **b** and all possible combinations of true and false.
3.   In columns *3* and *4* we translate the logical expression: Not (a Or b) into JavaScript operators: !(a || b).
4.   In columns *5*, *6*, and *7* we translate the logical expression: Not a And Not b into JavaScript operators: !a && !b
5.   We write the result of (a || b) in column *3*. We write column 3 before column 4 because a || b is inside parentheses.
6.   We write the result of !(a || b) in column *4* which finishes all the logic on the left side of the equivalency arrow (⇔).
7.   We write the result of !a in column *5*.
8.   We write the result of !b in column *6*.

Handbook for Beginning Programmers

9. In column 7 we combine columns 5 and 6 using && which finishes all the logic on the left side of the equivalency arrow (⇔).

10. Finally, we compare the results in columns 4 and 7 and because they are the same, we have proven that Not (a Or b) ⇔ Not a And Not b. In other words, we computed Not (a Or b) for all possible combinations of true and false, and we computed Not a And Not b for all possible combinations of true and false, and we found in all cases that the results were the same. Because Not (a Or b) always gives the same results as Not a And Not b, the two logical expressions are equivalent.

1	2	4	3		5	7	6
a	**b**	**!**	**(a || b)**	⇔	**!a**	**&&**	**!a**
False	False	True	False		True	True	True
False	True	False	True		True	False	False
True	False	False	True		False	False	True
True	True	False	True		False	False	False

Example 8

Given any two conditions *a* and *b*, show the result of (a And b) Xor Not (a Or b)

1	2	3	6	5	4
a	**b**	**(a && b)**	**^**	**!**	**(a || b)**

Example 9

Given any two conditions *a* and *b*, prove that Not (a And b) ⇔ Not a Or Not b

1	2	4	3		5	7	6
a	**b**	**!**	**(a && b)**	⇔	**!a**	**||**	**!b**

Example 10

Given any three conditions *a*, *b*, and *c*, prove (a Or b) Or c ⇔ a Or (b Or c)

1	2	3	4	5	7	6
a	**b**	**c**	**(a || b)**	**|| c**	**⇔ a ||**	**(b || c)**

Handbook for Beginning Programmers

Using De Morgan's Law

Your school desires to help average students improve their grades. You have been asked to write a program to print a list of students that are *not* on the dean's list for academic excellence. You know that the requirements for being on the dean's list are to have a GPA greater than 3.5 and have completed at least 32 credits. However, your program is supposed to print a list of all the students *not* on the dean's list. How can you write an `if` statement to decide to print a student's name or not? Start with the dean's list criteria:

```
if (gpa > 3.5 && credits >= 32) {
    document.getElementById('outputDiv').innerHTML =
            name + " is on the dean's list.";
}
```

The above code will print a student's name if the student qualifies for the dean's list. However, your program is supposed to print a list of all the students *not* on the dean's list. So, you simply add a Not (!) to negate or reverse the sense of the boolean expression.

```
if (!(gpa > 3.5 && credits >= 32)) {
    document.getElementById('outputDiv').innerHTML =
            name + ' is on the average list.';
}
```

This new `if` statement works but is a bit sloppy and not very understandable. You realize that the condition looks like the left half of De Morgan's law part b. So you decide to rewrite the condition. From De Morgan's law we see that Not (a And b) ⇔ Not a Or Not b, so you can rewrite the previous expression as:

```
if (!(gpa > 3.5) || !(credits >= 32)) {
    document.getElementById('outputDiv').innerHTML =
            name + ' is on the average list.';
}
```

Which can be simplified as:

```
if (gpa <= 3.5 || credits < 32) {
    document.getElementById('outputDiv').innerHTML =
            name + ' is on the average list.';
}
```

This final expression is simple to understand and correctly determines if a student is not on the dean's list.

Common Mistakes

Forgetting the left-hand side of a second comparison

Incorrect
```
if (y == 6 || 7) {
}
```

Correct
```
if (y == 6 || y == 7) {
}
```

```
if (y == (6 || 7)) {
}
```

```
if (y == 6, 7) {
}
```

```
if (y == (6, 7)) {
}
```

Forgetting &&

Incorrect
```
if (10 < x < 20) {
}
```

Correct
```
if (10 < x && x < 20) {
}
```

Mixing up the logical operators

Incorrect
```
// This will always be
// true. Think about it.
if (x > 10 || x < 20) {
}
```

Correct
```
// Almost certainly you
// meant to write this:
if (10 < x && x < 20) {
}
```

```
// This will always be
// false.
if (x == 8 && x == 9) {
}
```

```
// Almost certainly you
// meant to write this:
if (x == 8 || x == 9) {
}
```

Chapter Summary

- We can use the logical operators to combine multiple comparisons in the condition of a single `if` statement.
- The JavaScript logical operators are: Not (!), And (&&), Inclusive Or (||), and Exclusive Or (^).
- Not (!) has a higher precedence than the other logical operators because it is a unary operator.
- The logical operators can also be used in an online search to refine the results of the search. However, the logical And operator might not be explicitly written in the search query but may be implied by a space character.
- We can use logical equivalences to rewrite logical expressions in a way that is shorter or clearer.
- We can use a truth table to help us discover and prove logical equivalences.
- DeMorgan's laws are a group of four logical equivalences that are commonly used when rewriting logical expressions that include the Not logical operator.

Review Questions

1. Use advanced search at google (www.google.com/advanced_search) to find on the internet a recipe for pizza that doesn't include tomato sauce. Besides the dough, what ingredients does the recipe use?

2. Search the online gospel library at scriptures.lds.org to find the verses in the scriptures with the phrase "word of my power". Occasionally the search at scriptures.lds.org doesn't work. If that is the case, you could use the search at lds.org or the advanced search at google (www.google.com/advanced_search) and restrict your search to `site:scriptures.lds.org` How many **verses** did you find? Who is the "word of my power"?

Using a truth table, do the following.

3. (De Morgan's law) Prove that Not (a Or b) ⇔ Not a And Not b

4. Prove that Not (a Or b) <=/=> (Not a Or b)
   Note that the symbol <=/=> means not equivalent.

5. Write a truth table for this Boolean expression: (a Or b) And Not (a Xor b). Does the result seem familiar? Is it possible to rewrite this boolean expression more simply and get the same result? What is the simplified expression?

6. Write a truth table for this Boolean expression: (a And b) Xor Not (b Or c)

Programming Assignments

1. Write a defining table and then a program that reads from the keyboard a student's name and number of completed university credits and then outputs the student's name and year in school according to this table.

If the number of credits is greater than or equal to	And the number of credits is less than	Then the year in school is
0	30	freshman
30	60	sophomore
60	90	junior
90	∞	senior

2. Write a defining table and a program that asks the user to enter a month name (January, February, etc) and then outputs the number of days in the month. For February, output "28 or 29 days".

3. You work for a retail store that wants to increase sales on Tuesday and Wednesday which are the store's slowest sales days. Write a defining table and then a program that takes a customer's subtotal as input and if the subtotal is greater than $50 and today is Tuesday or Wednesday, subtracts 10% from the subtotal. Your program should then compute and output the total amount due by adding sales tax of 6% to the subtotal. Within your program, use this JavaScript code that will get the current day of the week from your computer's clock:

```
var dayOfWeek = new Date().getDay();
```

If you use the above code, the variable *dayOfWeek* will hold 0 if today is Sunday, 1 if today is Monday, and so on to 6 if today is Saturday.

4. Write a defining table and then a program that determines if you can sleep in or not. Your program should get all its input from your computer's clock. On all weekdays (Monday through Friday) that are not holidays, your program should output "Get up!" On all other days (weekends and holidays) your program should output "Sleep in." The three holidays that your program must check for are January 1 (New Year's Day), July 4 (U.S. Independence Day), and December 25 (Christmas). You don't need to include other holidays in your program because most other holidays do not occur on a fixed day each year.

Within your program, use this JavaScript code that will get the current month, current day of the month, and current day of the week from your computer's clock:

```
var now = new Date();
var month = now.getMonth();
var dayOfMonth = now.getDate();
var dayOfWeek = now.getDay();
```

If you use the above code, the variable *month* will hold 0 if the current month is January, 1 if February, and so on to 11 if December. The variable *dayOfMonth* will hold 1 for the first day of the month up to 28, 29, 30, or 31 for the last day of the month. The variable *dayOfWeek* will hold 0 if today is Sunday, 1 if today is Monday, and so on to 6 if today is Saturday.

Chapter 8. Repetition

A computer programmer can cause a computer to repeat a series of statements by writing a loop in a computer program. Every loop includes a boolean condition. Each time the computer needs to decide if it should repeat the statements inside a loop, the computer evaluates the loop's condition. If the condition evaluates to true, then the computer repeats the statements inside the loop. If the condition evaluates to false, the computer does not repeat the inside statements but instead continues executing the program starting with the statements after the loop.

Chapter Outcomes

By the end of this chapter you will:

- Be able to distinguish between pre-test and post-test loops and between counting and sentinel controlled loops.
- Know when to use a pre-test or post-test loop and when to use a counting or sentinel controlled loop.
- Be able to read and write while, for, and do-while loops that cause a computer to repeat a group of statements.
- Know what the keyword break inside a loop causes a computer to do.

Pre-test and Post-test Loops

Loops can be categorized according to where the boolean condition is located. A **pre-test loop** has the condition at the top of the loop. It is known as a pre-test loop because the condition is evaluated *before* (pre) the computer executes the statements inside the loop. A **post-test loop** has the condition at the bottom of the loop. It is called a post-test loop because the condition is evaluated *after* (post) the statements inside the loop are executed.

With a pre-test loop, the statements inside the loop may never be executed. This is because when the computer encounters the loop, the first thing the computer will do is to evaluate the loop's condition. If the condition evaluates to false, then the statements inside the loop will not be executed.

With a post-test loop, the statements inside the loop will always be executed at least once because when the computer encounters the loop, it will first execute the statements inside the loop, and then it will evaluate the loop's condition.

Pre-test loops are used much more frequently than post-test loops. In fact all post-test loops can be rewritten as pre-test loops, so post-test loops are not strictly necessary in a programming language, but they are sometimes convenient to use.

Counting and Sentinel Controlled Loops

Loops can also be categorized by what is in their condition. A **counting loop** causes the computer to count from a start value to an end value. A counting loop's condition is a simple check to see if the counting variable has reached the end value. A **sentinel controlled loop** causes the computer to repeat statements until some event occurs or the computer encounters some sentinel value. A sentinel controlled loop's condition checks for the occurrence of that event or that sentinel value.

Repetition Control Structures

JavaScript has four different ways to write a repetition control structure to cause a computer to repeat statements. The four ways are: while, for, for-each, and do-while. The while, for, and for-each loops are pre-test loops. The do-while loop is a post-test loop. The while, for, and do-while loops all have a condition and repeat the statements inside of them while the condition is true. The for-each loop repeats the statements inside the loop once for each attribute in an object.

while

Use a while loop when:
- You need a simple counting loop; or
- You can't use a simple counting loop, so you must use a sentinel controlled loop, and the sentinel must be checked before executing the statements inside the loop.

Template

```
while (condition) {
    statements;
}
```

Figure 26 shows a while loop and the order in which the computer executes its parts.

```
var i = 1;
while (i < 3) {
    window.alert(i);
    i++;
}
```

Figure 26: A while loop and the order that the computer executes its parts.

Example 1

```
var i = 1;
while (i < 3) {
    // Statements to be repeated go here.
    window.alert(i);
    i++;
}
```

Desk Check

i

for

The for loop is a shortened way of writing a counting while loop. Use a for loop when:

- You need a simple counting loop.

Template

```
for (initialization; condition; update) {
    statements;
}
```

Within the parentheses of a for loop there must always be three statements separated by two semicolons. The three statements are:

1. The initialization statement which is executed only once at the beginning of the loop.
2. The condition that the computer checks to see if it should continue to execute the statements inside the body of the loop. The computer checks this condition after the initialization statement and each time at the beginning of the loop.
3. The update statement that the computer executes each time through the loop as if it were written as the last statement in the body of the loop.

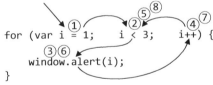

Figure 27: A for loop and the order that the computer executes its parts.

Figure 27 shows a for loop and the order in which the computer executes the statements in the parentheses and the body.

Example 2

```
for (var i = 1;  i < 3;  i++) {
    // Statements to be repeated go here.
    window.alert(i);
}
```

Desk Check

i

Within the parentheses of a for loop there must always be three statements separated by two semicolons. You may leave any or all of the statements blank, but you must always include the two semicolons as shown in example 3.

Example 3

```
var i = parseInt(
        document.getElementById('startInputBox').value);
for ( ;  i <= 5;  i++) {
    // Statements to be repeated go here.
    window.alert(i);
}
```

Desk Check

i
4

For Each Loop

The for-each loop is a special case of the for loop. The for-each loop causes the statements inside of it to be repeated once for each attribute in an object. Use a for-each loop when:

- The statements in the loop must be repeated once for each element in an array or collection.

Template

```
for (variable in object) {
    statements;
}
```

Example 4

```
var text = '';
for (var part in document) {
    // Statements to be repeated go here.
    text += part + ': ' + document[part] + '<br>';
}
document.getElementById('outputDiv').innerHTML = text;
```

do while

The do-while loop is the only post-test loop in JavaScript. The other three loops: while, for, and for-each are pre-test loops.

Use when:

- You can't use a simple counting loop, so you must use a sentinel controlled loop; and
- The statements inside the loop must be executed before checking the sentinel.

Template

```
do {
    statements;
} while (condition);
```

Figure 28 shows a do-while loop and the order in which the computer executes its parts. The statements in a post-test loop will always be executed at least once because the test to continue the loop is at the bottom and is evaluated after the statements in the body are executed. The statements in a pre-test loop (while, for, and for-each) may never be executed because the test is at the top of those loops and evaluated before the statements in the body.

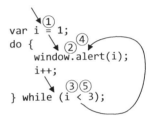

Figure 28: A do-while loop and the order that the computer executes its parts.

Example 5

```
var alias, response;
do {
    // Statements to be repeated go here.
    alias = window.prompt("What is your name?");
    response = window.prompt("Are you sure " +
        alias + " is your name?");
} while (response != "yes");
window.alert("Hello " + alias);
```

Desk Check

alias	response

Zero-Based Counting Loop

Experienced computer programmers almost always write counting loops to begin at zero (0) rather than one (1) as we have all been taught since before kindergarten. There are probably many reasons programmers start loops at zero; one of them is because array elements (see chapter 10) are indexed starting with zero in C, C++, Java, and JavaScript. Because zero-based counting loops are so common and useful in computer programming, the aspiring programmer must learn them. Below are two examples of zero-based counting loops that execute the statements inside the loops exactly *n* times.

Example 6

```
var n = 3;
var i = 0;
while (i < n) {
    window.alert("leaf");
    i++;
}
```

Desk Check

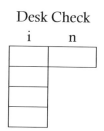

Example 7

```
var n = 3;
for (var i = 0;  i < n;  i++) {
    window.alert("caterpillar");
}
```

Desk Check

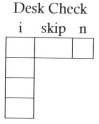

Skipping Loop

Sometimes we want the computer to count by a value other than 1. We can write a loop that will cause the computer to skip values.

Example 8

```
var skip = 4;
var n = 12;
var i = 0;
while (i < n) {
    window.alert("stem");
    i += skip;
}
```

Desk Check

i   skip   n

Example 9

```
var skip = 2;
var n = 5;
for (var i = 0;  i < n;  i += skip) {
    window.alert("aphid");
}
```

Infinite Loop

What does the computer do if a programmer forgets to write the update part of a loop? For example:

```
var i = 0;
while (i < 5) {
    window.alert('Hello');
}
```

Or this example:

```
for (var i = 0;  i < 5;  ) {
    window.alert('Hello');
}
```

Notice in both examples that after the value of the counting variable *i* is initialized to zero (0), its value is never changed. This means that *i* will start at the value zero (0), and each time the computer evaluates the continuation condition (i < 5), *i* will be less than 5. In other words, the continuation condition will always evaluate to true and the computer will keep repeating the statements inside the loop forever or until the user kills the program. This is called an **infinite loop** and is usually, although not always, a mistake. Of course the way to fix both of the above infinite loop examples is to add code to change the value of *i* within the body of the loops, for example:

```
var i = 0;
while (i < 5) {
    window.alert('Hello');
    i++;
}

for (var i = 0;  i < 5;  i += 2) {
    window.alert('Hello');
}
```

Repetitive Strings

Occasionally we need the computer to produce a string that has a repeating pattern. We can use a loop to cause the computer to build such strings. Consider the string "0, 2, 4, 6, 8, 10" with the simple pattern of counting by twos. Here is code that builds this string and displays it to the user.

Example 10

```
var output = '0';
var i = 2;
while (i <= 10) {
    output += ', ' + i;
    i += 2;
}
document.getElementById('displayDiv').innerHTML = output;
```

Notice in the above code that the line

```
output += ', ' + i;
```

performs string concatenation and not addition. This is because the starting value for the variable *output* is a string ('0') and because the comma and space (', ') is also a string. The += operator for string concatenation will append new text onto the string each time through the loop so that the value in *output* will grow from '0' to '0, 2' to '0, 2, 4' etc.

Desk Check

i	output

Compound Interest

Many bank accounts and other investments pay compound interest on the money that is saved in the account. This means each time the bank pays interest, the interest is added to the original money, which is called the principal. Then the next time the bank pays interest, it pays interest on the principal and the previous interest. The balance of such an account and its compound interest can easily be computed using a loop.

Example 11

```
<!DOCTYPE HTML>
<html lang="en-us">
<head>
<meta charset="utf-8">
<title>Compound Interest</title>

<script type="text/javascript">
/* Input:
 *     An amount to invest: balance
 *     The annual rate of growth: annualRate
 *     The number of months to invest: numMonths
 * Processing: Use a loop to compute the balance of the account after
 *      a bank has paid interest paid for numMonths number of months.
 * Output: The balance after numMonths have passed.
 */
function futureValue() {
    var balance = parseFloat(document.getElementById('balance').value);
    var annualRate =parseFloat(document.getElementById('annualRate').value);
    var numMonths = parseInt(document.getElementById('months').value);
    var monthlyRate = annualRate / 12;

    // For each month, compute the interest and add it to the balance.
    for (var month = 1;  month <= numMonths;  month++) {
        // Compute the interest for a month.
        var interest = balance * monthlyRate;

        // Round the interest to pennies.
        interest = Math.round(interest * 100) / 100;

        // Add the interest to the balance.
        balance += interest;
    }
    document.getElementById('output').innerHTML =
        "Your balance after " + numMonths + " months will be $" + balance;
}
</script>
</head>
```

```
<body>
Balance: <input type="text" id="balance" size="7"><br>
Annual growth rate: <input type="text" id="annualRate" size="5"><br>
Number of months: <input type="text" id="months" size="3"><br>
<button type="button" onclick="futureValue()">Future Value</button>
<div id="output"></div>
</body>
</html>
```

Desk Check

annualRate	monthlyRate	numMonths	month	interest	balance
0.06		3			100

break

The break keyword causes the computer to end a loop prematurely. It is normally used inside an if statement that is inside a loop. Here is a code example that reads 10 or fewer numbers from a user and computes and outputs the sum of those numbers. The code stops reading numbers from the user after 10 numbers or after the user enters zero (0), whichever comes first.

Example 12

```
// Gets 10 or fewer numbers from the user and adds them together.
function sum10() {
    var sum = 0;
    for (var i = 0;  i < 10;  i++) {
        var n = parseFloat(window.prompt('Please enter a number'));
        if (n == 0) {
            break;
        }
        sum += n;
    }
    window.alert(sum);
}
```

Desk Check

i	n	sum
	17	
	−3	
	6	
	0	

Prime Numbers

A prime number is a positive integer that is evenly divisible by only two integers, 1 and itself. The numbers 2, 3, 5, and 7 are prime as are 91, 97, and 101. Prime numbers are very important in computing, for example in hash code algorithms and data encryption. There are many well know algorithms, including the sieve of Eratosthenes, for determining if a number is prime. The following JavaScript code uses a naive and slow algorithm to determine if a number is prime, but it works. The code below increments a divisor from 1 to the candidate number, inclusive and repeatedly divides the candidate by the divisor. Each time the divisor divides the candidate without a remainder, then a factor count is incremented. After the divisor loop is finished, if the factor count is 2 (1 and the candidate itself), the candidate is prime, otherwise it is not prime.

Example 13

```
<!DOCTYPE HTML>
<html lang="en-us">
<head>
<meta charset="utf-8">
<title>Prime Number</title>

<script type="text/javascript">
/* Input: an integer
 * Processing: determine if the given integer is prime or not.
 * Output: __ is prime OR __ is not prime */
function isPrime() {
    var candidate = parseInt(document.getElementById('integerBox').value);

    // Count the number of factors that evenly divide candidate
    var factorCount = 0;
    for (var divisor = 1;  divisor <= candidate;  divisor++) {
        var remainder = candidate % divisor;
        if (remainder == 0) {
            factorCount++;
        }
    }

    // Determine the output and show it to the user.
    var output;
    if (factorCount == 2) {
        output = candidate + ' is prime';
    }
    else {
        output = candidate + ' is not prime';
    }
    document.getElementById('outputDiv').innerHTML = output;
```

```
}
</script>
</head>

<body>
Please enter an integer: <input type="text" id="integerBox"><br>
<button type="button" onclick="isPrime()">Is Prime</button>
<div id="outputDiv"></div>
</body>
</html>
```

Desk Check

candidate	divisor	remainder	factorCount	output
8				

The algorithm used by the previous code is naive and slow. What improvements could be made to the code to speed it up?

Example 14 contains a different version of the isPrime code that includes three improvements.

1. The divisor loop begins counting at 2 instead of 1.
2. The divisor loop no longer counts factors, but instead ends as soon as the computer determines the candidate number is not prime.
3. In the case of a prime number, the divisor loop does not count all the way to the candidate number but stops at the square root of the candidate number.

Handbook for Beginning Programmers

Example 14

```
<!DOCTYPE HTML>
<html lang="en-us">
<head>
<meta charset="utf-8">
<title>Prime Number</title>

<script type="text/javascript">
/* Input: an integer
 * Processing: determine if the given integer is prime or not.
 * Output: __ is prime OR __ is not prime */
function isPrime() {
    var candidate = parseInt(document.getElementById('integerBox').value);
    var limit = Math.sqrt(candidate);
    var isPrime = true;
    for (var divisor = 2;  divisor <= limit;  divisor++) {
        var remainder = candidate % divisor;
        if (remainder == 0) {
            isPrime = false;
            break;
        }
    }

    // Determine the output and show it to the user.
    var output;
    if (isPrime) {
        output = candidate + ' is prime';
    }
    else {
        output = candidate + ' is not prime';
    }
    document.getElementById('outputDiv').innerHTML = output;
}
</script>
</head>

<body>
Please enter an integer: <input type="text" id="integerBox"><br>
<button type="button" onclick="isPrime()">Is Prime</button>
<div id="outputDiv"></div>
</body>
</html>
```

Desk Check

candidate	limit	isPrime	divisor	remainder	output
8					

Common Mistakes

Writing an infinite loop

Incorrect
```
var i = 0;
while (i < 3) {
    window.alert("Hello");
}
```

Correct
```
var i = 0;
while (i < 3) {
    window.alert("Hello");
    i++;
}

// or

for (var i = 0; i < 3; i++) {
    window.alert("Hello");
}
```

Writing a loop that never repeats

Incorrect
```
for (var i = 0; i > 3; i++) {
}
```

Correct
```
for (var i = 0; i < 3; i++) {
}

// or

for (var i= 0; i != 3; i++) {
}
```

Using commas to separate the parts of a for loop

Incorrect
```
for (var i = 0, i < 5, i++) {
}
```

Correct
```
for (var i = 0; i < 5; i++) {
}
```

Forgetting braces when there is more than one statement inside a loop

Incorrect
```
for (var i = 0; i < n; i++)
    interest = balance * rate;
    balance += interest;
```

Correct
```
for (var i = 0; i < n; i++) {
    interest = balance * rate;
    balance += interest;
}
```

Handbook for Beginning Programmers

Placing a semicolon at the end of a while loop or for loop

Incorrect
```
var i = 0;
while (i < 3); {
    window.alert("Hello");
    i++;
}

for (var i = 0; i < 3; i++); {
    window.alert("Hello");
}
```

Correct
```
var i = 0;
while (i < 3) {
    window.alert("Hello");
    i++;
}

for (var i = 0; i < 3; i++) {
    window.alert("Hello");
}
```

Chapter Summary

- Repetition is the control structure that a programmer uses to cause a computer to repeat a group of statements.
- Loop is the informal term for repetition control structure.
- In a pre-test loop, the loop continuation condition is written at the top of the loop which causes a computer to check the condition before the computer executes the statements in the loop.
- In a post-test loop, the loop continuation condition is written at the bottom of the loop which causes a computer to execute the statements in the loop before it checks the condition.
- A counting loop causes a computer to repeat a group of statements until a counting variable reaches a desired number.
- A sentinel controlled loop causes a computer to repeat a group of statements until an event (the sentinel) occurs.
- There are four styles of loops in JavaScript: while, for, for-each, and do-while.
- A while loop is a pre-test loop that is often used as a sentinel controlled loop that causes a computer to repeat the statements inside it while a given condition is true.
- A for loop is a pre-test loop that is used for writing simple counting loops.
- A do-while loop is a post-test loop that is often used as a sentinel controlled loop.

Review Questions

1. Write a loop to count by threes from zero to nine. After the loop is finished, your counting variable should hold the value 9.

2. Write a loop to count backwards from 90 to 81. After the loop is finished, your counting variable should hold the value 81.

3. Write a loop to count forwards by twos from the value in the variable first to the value in the variable last. Assume the variables first and last already exist and hold values.

4. Write a loop to count backwards by twos from the value in the variable last to the value in the variable first. Assume the variables last and first already exist and hold values.

5. Desk check the following code and then write a sentence describing what the code does.

```
function func1() {
    var c = "";
 var a = parseInt(document.getElementById('integerBox').value);
    var b = 100;
        while (b >= 0) {
 c += b + "<br>";
        b -= a;
            }
    document.getElementById('outputDiv').innerHTML = c;
}
```

Desk Check

a	b	c
20		

6. Desk check the following code and then write a sentence describing what the code does. How does this code differ from the code in the previous example? Hint: consider the indentation of the statements in the previous example compared to the indentation of the statements in this example. Which example is easier to read and desk check?

```
function func2() {
    var c = "";
    var a = parseInt(document.getElementById('integerBox').value);
    var b = 100;
    while (b >= 0) {
        c += b + "<br>";
        b -= a;
    }
    document.getElementById('outputDiv').innerHTML = c;
}
```

Desk Check

a	b	c
20		

7. Desk check the following code and then write a sentence describing what the code does. How does this code differ from the code in the previous two examples?

```javascript
function countDown() {
    var output = "";
    var skip = parseInt(document.getElementById('integerBox').value);
    var i = 100;
    while (i >= 0) {
        output += i + "<br>";
        i -= skip;
    }
    document.getElementById('outputDiv').innerHTML = output;
}
```

Desk Check

skip	i	output
20		

8. Desk check the following code and then write a sentence describing what the code does.

```
function func4() {
      var d = "Please enter an integer.";
var b = 38;
    var c;
  do {
       c = parseInt(window.prompt(d));
      if (c < b) {
      d = "Too low. Please enter another integer.";
           }
      else if (c > b) {
d = "Too high. Please enter another integer.";
}
      } while (c != b);
  window.alert(c + " is correct!");
}
```

Desk Check

b	c	d

9. Desk check the following code and then write a sentence describing what the code does. How does this code differ from the code in the previous example? Hint: consider the indentation of the statements in the previous example compared to the indentation of the statements in this example. Which example is easier to read and desk check?

```
function func5() {
    var d = "Please enter an integer.";
    var b = 38;
    var c;
    do {
        c = parseInt(window.prompt(d));
        if (c < b) {
            d = "Too low. Please enter another integer.";
        }
        else if (c > b) {
            d = "Too high. Please enter another integer.";
        }
    } while (c != b);
    window.alert(c + " is correct!");
}
```

Desk Check

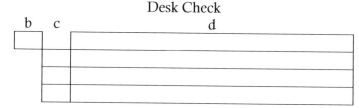

b	c	d

Handbook for Beginning Programmers

10. Desk check the following code and then write a sentence describing what the code does. How does this code differ from the code in the previous two examples?

```
function numberGuessGame() {
    var message =
        "I'm thinking of a number between 1 and 100.\n" +
        "Try to guess it!\n" +
        "Please enter an integer between 1 and 100.";
    var answer = 38;
    var guess;
    do {
        guess = parseInt(window.prompt(message));
        if (guess < answer) {
            message = guess +
                " is too low. Please enter another integer.";
        }
        else if (guess > answer) {
            message = guess +
                " is too high. Please enter another integer.";
        }
    } while (guess != answer);
    message = guess + " is correct!";
    window.alert(message);
}
```

Desk Check

answer	guess	message

Programming Assignments

1. Write a defining table and a program that asks the user for an integer n and then outputs all the integers between 1 and n, inclusive.

2. Write a defining table and a program that asks the user for an integer n and then outputs the sum of all the odd integers between 1 and n, inclusive.

3. Write a defining table and a program to print the five times table from 1 to 12 in this format:
    5 x 1 = 5
    5 x 2 = 10
    ...
    5 x 12 = 60

4. Write a defining table and a program to print all powers of 2 from 2^0 up to 2^{31}, inclusive. In other words, your program should output this series:
    1, 2, 4, 8, ... 2147483648

5. Write a defining table and a program that outputs the first 25 numbers in this Fibonacci series: 0, 1, 1, 2, 3, 5, 8...

6. Rewrite the number guessing game code found in review question 10 so that it counts the number of guesses the user takes to correctly guess the answer.

7. Write a defining table and a program that asks the user for an integer n and then outputs the following table.

n	2*n	3*n	n*n	n*n*n
1	2	3	1	1
2	4	6	4	8
3	6	9	9	27
⋮	⋮	⋮	⋮	⋮
n	$2n$	$3n$	n^2	n^3

8. Write a defining table and a program that allows a user to enter ten numbers and then computes and outputs the average of those numbers. The user interface for your program should look similar to Figure 29. Your program must use a loop to read the ten numbers and compute the sum of those numbers.

9. Write a defining table and a program that prints a 12 by 12 multiplication table.

Figure 29: An HTML document and JavaScript program that computes the average of ten numbers.

Chapter 9. Functions

Because most useful computer programs are very large, computer programmers divide their programs into parts. A part of a program is called a **module**. In JavaScript the smallest module that performs actions is a **function**, which is sometimes called a **method**. Nearly all statements in a JavaScript program must be written inside a function.

The term function comes from mathematics and is the name of the concept that one value (the **argument** of the function) completely determines another value (the **result** of the function). Consider the function f with one argument x : $f(x) = 2x - 1$. We can substitute any number for the argument x which completely determines the result of the function f. For example, substituting 5 for x produces 9 as the result of the function: $f(5) = 2(5) - 1 = 9$. Functions in a computer program work in a similar way, taking arguments and producing results.

Chapter Outcomes

By the end of this chapter you will:

- Write functions that accept and use parameters.
- Write code to return a value from a function to its call point.
- Write code to call a function and pass arguments to that function.
- Write code to store the result returned from a function in a variable.
- Distinguish between a parameter and an argument.
- Distinguish between displaying output for the user to see and returning a value to be used by the program.
- Understand local variable scope.

Writing a Function

To write a function in JavaScript, simply type code that matches this template.

Template

```
function functionName(param1, param2, … paramN) {
    statements;
    return value;
}
```

The first line of a function is called the **header** or **signature**, and it includes

1. the keyword function
2. the function name
3. the parameter list

The function name must start with a letter, the underscore (_), or the dollar sign ($). The rest of the name must be made of letters, digits (0–9), the underscore, or the dollar sign. A function name cannot include spaces. It should be a meaningful name that curtly describes what the function does. The **parameter list** contains data stored in variables that the function needs to complete its task.

The statements inside a function are called the **body** of the function. A function may contain as many statements as you wish to write inside of it. However, it is a good idea to limit functions to less than a page (60 lines) long. To **return** a result from a function so that the result can be used somewhere else in your program, simply type the keyword return followed by whatever value you want returned to the calling function.

Example 1

Write the header for a function named drawCircle that takes three parameters: the x and y values for the center of the circle and the radius of the circle, all in pixels.

```
function drawCircle(centerX, centerY, radius)
```

Example 2

Write the header for a function named getDiscountRate which returns the discount rate applied to a student's car insurance premium. The function requires two parameters: the student's birthday and GPA.

Why does the getDiscountRate function require two parameters? In other words, what rule does the insurance company have that requires getDiscountRate to have two parameters?

Example 3

Write a function (header and body) that computes and returns the average of three numbers.

```
// Computes and returns the average of three numbers.
function average(a, b, c) {
    var sum = a + b + c;
    var avg = sum / 3;
    return avg;
}
```

Handbook for Beginning Programmers

Example 4

Write a function that takes two parameters and computes and returns the value of this equation: $f(a,r) = a \times (1 + r)$.

Calling a Function

Calling or **invoking** a function causes the computer to execute the code in that function. If you write a function, but never write a call to that function, then the code in that function will never be executed. To call a function, simply write its name followed by the data, known as **arguments**, which the function will need to perform its task. An argument can be a constant such as 23, a string literal such as 'Idaho', or a variable. If you use variables as arguments in a function call, the names of the arguments do not have to match the names of the parameters. However, the order of the arguments must match the order of the parameters.

Template

```
functionName(arg1, arg2, … argN);
```

Example 5

Write the code to call a function that has this header:

```
function drawCircle(centerX, centerY, radius)

function run() {
    var x = parseInt(document.getElementById('xInputBox').value);
    var y = parseInt(document.getElementById('yInputBox').value);
    var radius = parseInt(document.getElementById('radiusInputBox').value);
    drawCircle(x, y, radius);
}
```

Example 6

Write code to call a function that has this header:

```
function drawRectangle(x, y, width, height)
```

To call a function *and* assign its result to a variable so the result can be used later, write a line that includes the variable name that will hold the result, the assignment operator (=), the function name, and the arguments to the function.

Template

```
varName = functionName(arg1, arg2, … argN);
```

Example 7

Write code to call the square root function found in the Math object and assign the result returned from it to a variable named *rt*. The square root function has this header:

```
function sqrt(x)
```

```
function testSqrt() {
    var value = 73.1;
    var rt = Math.sqrt(value);
    document.getElementById('outputDiv').innerHTML = rt;
}
```

Example 8

Write code to call a function named computeCaloriesBurned and store the result returned from the function in a variable named *calories*. The function has this header:

```
function computeCaloriesBurned(distance, elevation, weight)
```

Figure 30 demonstrates what the computer does when it executes a function call. As shown in the diagram, the computer copies the value of each argument into the corresponding parameter and then executes the code in the function. When it is finished executing the code inside the function, the computer returns a value to the **call point**. At the call point, the returned value may be stored in a variable or used in an arithmetic expression.

Figure 30: Demonstration of a function call, showing how the arguments are assigned to the parameters and showing that when the computer is finished executing the function, the result is returned from the function to the call point.

Variable Scope

The **scope** of a variable determines how long that variable exists and where it can be used. Within a JavaScript program, there are two categories of scope: local and global. A **local variable** is declared inside a function, exists for as long as its containing function is executing, and can be used within its containing function only. A **global variable** is declared outside all functions, exists for as long as its containing file is loaded in the computer's memory, and can be used within all functions in its containing file. Parameters are local variables because they are declared within a function, specifically within a function's header.

JavaScript Variable Scope

	Local	Global
Where to Declare	Inside a function	Outside all functions
Owner	The function where the variable is declared	The JavaScript program, or stated more accurately, the HTML file that contains the script tag where it is declared
Lifetime	Only as long as its containing function is executing	As long as its containing HTML file is loaded in the computer's memory
Where Usable	Only inside the function where it is declared	In all functions in the JavaScript program

Because local variables are visible only within the function where they are declared, you can declare two variables with the same name as long as they are declared in different functions. In the example code below there are two functions each with a local variable named *length* and a local variable named *area*. The variables are entirely separate and do not conflict in any way because the scope of each variable is within the function where it is declared.

Example 9

```
function squareArea(length) {
    var area = length * length;
    return area;
}

function rectangleArea(width, length) {
    var area = width * length;
    return area;
}
```

Advantages of Functions

There are multiple advantages to writing statements inside a function instead of outside of all functions, including

1. Control of execution – JavaScript statements that are inside an HTML script tag but outside of all functions are executed immediately when a document is read into memory by a browser. Statements that are inside a function are not executed until a function is called which gives the programmer control over when those statements are executed.
2. Code reuse – After a function is written it can be reused again and again by calling it from multiple locations in a program.
3. Less code – Because a programmer can reuse code, he does not have to write as much code.
4. Fewer coding mistakes – writing less code will naturally lead to fewer mistakes because there is simply less code to contain the mistakes.
5. Better organization
6. Easier to read and understand
7. Easier to debug
8. Faster execution – Because a program with well written functions contains less code, that program will very likely load faster and execute faster.
9. Variable name reuse – Because variables declared inside a function are local to that function only, a programmer can reuse variable names in different functions.

Summary of Terms

module
: a part of a program; can refer to a very large part of a program, including many files and functions, or can refer to a small part of a program such as a single function

function
: the smallest part of a program that performs actions, sometimes called a **method**; also the JavaScript keyword that begins a function

header
: the first line of a function; also known as the **signature**; includes the function name and parameter list

parameter
: a piece of data that a function needs in order to complete its task or perform its calculations; parameters are listed in a function's header

body
: the part of a function that contains the JavaScript code that is executed when a function is called; the code in a function's body produces the result or return value of that function

call point	a location in a program where a function is called or invoked
argument	the actual value that is passed into a function when the function is called; arguments are listed at the call point of a function
variable scope	the part of a program where a variable can be used; also determines how long a variable exists in the computer's memory
return	the JavaScript keyword that terminates a function and returns a value to the call point of the function

Pseudo Random Integer

The following code example shows how to obtain a pseudo random integer that is in the range *min* inclusive to *max* exclusive, in other words in the range [*min*, *max*). Notice that this code calls both the random and floor functions from the Math object.

Example 10

```
var r = min + Math.floor(Math.random() * (max - min));
```

Desk Check

min	max	value returned from Math.random	r
5	11	0.483	

Code Reuse

The most reusable functions are ones that perform only calculations and do not perform input and output. Chapter 6 contains code to determine if an integer is even or odd. Examples 11 and 12 below contain the same code split into two functions: doInputOutput and isEven. The first function gets the user input, calls the second function, and displays the result to the user. The first function is certainly useful in this program but is not reusable in another program because it requires a text field with an id of "number" and a div with an id of "output". The second function does only one thing: determine if an integer is even or odd. Because the second function does only calculations (it does not get user input nor display results to the user), the second function is reusable in other programs. The second function can be used in any program that needs to determine if an integer is even or odd regardless of where the input comes from, a user or a file or anywhere else.

Example 11

```
<!DOCTYPE HTML>
<html lang="en-us">
<head>
<meta charset="utf-8">
<title>Is Even</title>

<script type="text/javascript">
/* Input: An integer
 * Processing: Determine if the integer is even or not
 * Output: A message stating if the integer is even or not
 */
function doInputOutput() {
    var number = parseInt(document.getElementById('numberInputBox').value);
    var result = isEven(number);
    document.getElementById('outputDiv').innerHTML =
        number + ' is even: ' + result;
}

// Returns true if value is an even
// integer; otherwise returns false.
function isEven(value) {
    if ((value % 2) == 0) {
        return true;
    }
    else {
        return false;
    }
}
</script>
</head>
<body>
Please enter an integer: <input type="text" id="numberInputBox">
<button type="button" onclick="doInputOutput()">Is Even?</button>
<div id="outputDiv"></div>
</body>
</html>
```

Deck Check

number	result
8	

value	value % 2	return

Because the isEven function returns a boolean value, we can write it without the if statement. Eliminating the if statement makes the function easier to test because the function will contain only one possible path of execution instead of two.

Example 12

```
<!DOCTYPE HTML>
<html lang="en-us">
<head>
<meta charset="utf-8">
<title>Is Even</title>

<script type="text/javascript">
/* Input: An integer
 * Processing: Determine if the integer is even or not
 * Output: A message stating if the integer is even or not
 */
function doInputOutput() {
    var number = parseInt(document.getElementById('numberInputBox').value);
    var result = isEven(number);
    document.getElementById('outputDiv').innerHTML =
        number + ' is even: ' + result;
}

// Returns true if value is an even
// integer; otherwise returns false.
function isEven(value) {
    return (value % 2) == 0;
}
</script>
</head>

<body>
Please enter an integer: <input type="text" id="numberInputBox">
<button type="button" onclick="doInputOutput()">Is Even?</button>
<div id="outputDiv"></div>
</body>
</html>
```

Deck Check

number	result
8	

value	value % 2	return

Area of a Triangle

If we know the side lengths of a triangle as shown in Figure 31, we can compute the area of that triangle using **Heron's formula** which is

$$area = \sqrt{s(s-a)(s-b)(s-c)}$$

where a, b, and c are the lengths of the three sides of the triangle and s is the semi-perimeter of the triangle defined by

$$s = \frac{a+b+c}{2}$$

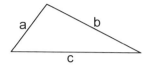

Figure 31: An irregular triangle with side lengths a, b, and c.

Example 13

```
<!DOCTYPE HTML>
<html lang="en-us">
<head>
<meta charset="utf-8">
<title>Triangle Area</title>

<script type="text/javascript">
/* Input: No user input
 * Processing: Compute the area of a triangle with side lengths 4, 2, and 5
 * Output: The area of the triangle
 */
function testTriangle() {
    var r = triangleArea(4, 2, 5);
    document.getElementById('outputDiv').innerHTML = r;
}

// Computes and returns the area of a
// triangle with side lengths a, b, and c.
function triangleArea(a, b, c) {
    var s = (a + b + c) / 2;
    var area = Math.sqrt(s * (s-a) * (s-b) * (s-c));
    return area;
}
</script>
</head>
<body>
<button type="button" onclick="testTriangle()">Test</button>
<div id="outputDiv"></div>
</body>
</html>
```

Desk Check

r

a	b	c	s	$(s-a)$	$(s-b)$	$(s-c)$	area

Handbook for Beginning Programmers

Surface Area of a Pyramid

Imagine designing one of the great pyramids. The stones on the inside of the pyramids are very rough and are basically just filler. The stones on the outside are finished smooth to reflect sunlight. If you were writing the software to design a pyramid, your software would have to compute the surface area of a pyramid so the builders would know how much finished stone they need to cover the outside of the pyramid.

Figure 32 shows a regular pyramid (all four sides are the same size) with edge length e, height h, and base length b. Since it is a regular pyramid, to compute the surface area your software could compute the area of one of the pyramid's triangular faces and multiply that by 4. If the builder of a regular pyramid specified the base length and the height, then your software could use this formula for computing the edge length from the base length and height:

Figure 32: A regular pyramid with edge length e, height h, and base length b.

$$e = \sqrt{\frac{b^2}{2} + h^2}$$

and then call the triangleArea function shown above to compute the area of one of the triangular faces.

Example 14

```
<!DOCTYPE HTML>
<html lang="en-us">
<head>
<meta charset="utf-8">
<title>Surface Area of a Pyramid</title>

<script type="text/javascript">
/* Input: No user input
 * Processing: Compute the surface area of the triangular faces
 *      of a regular pyramid that has base 8 and height 7.
 * Output: The surface area of the pyramid
 */
function testPyramid() {
    var pa = pyramidSurfaceArea(8, 7);
    document.getElementById('outputDiv').innerHTML = pa;
}

// Computes and returns the surface area of the
// four triangular faces of a regular pyramid
// with the specified base length and height.
function pyramidSurfaceArea(base, height) {
    var edge = Math.sqrt(base*base/2 + height*height);
    var triArea = triangleArea(base, edge, edge);
    var pyramidArea = 4 * triArea;
    return pyramidArea;
}

// Computes and returns the area of a
// triangle with side lengths a, b, and c.
function triangleArea(a, b, c) {
    var s = (a + b + c) / 2;
    var area = Math.sqrt(s * (s-a) * (s-b) * (s-c));
    return area;
}
</script>
</head>

<body>
<button type="button" onclick="testPyramid()">Test</button>
<div id="outputDiv"></div>
</body>
</html>
```

Desk Check

pa

base	height	edge	triArea	pyramidArea

a	b	c	s	$(s-a)$	$(s-b)$	$(s-c)$	area

How Long to Invest

A common question when saving and investing money is, "How long will I need to invest a certain amount of money in order for that money to grow to a certain larger amount of money?" For example, how many months will I need to invest $100 at 6% fixed annual growth rate compounded monthly in order for my investment to grow to $103?

Example 15

```
<!DOCTYPE HTML>
<html lang="en-us">
<head>
<meta charset="utf-8">
<title>How Long to Invest</title>
<script type="text/javascript">
/* Input: No user input
 * Processing: Determine the number of months required to grow an initial
 *   investment of $100 to at least $103 if it grows at an annual rate of 6%.
 * Output: The number of months. */
function testInvest() {
    var m = determineMonths(100, 0.06, 103);
    document.getElementById('outputDiv').innerHTML = m;
}
```

Desk Check

m

```
// Computes and returns the number of months needed for principal
// invested at a constant annual rate to grow to a target amount.
function determineMonths(principal, annualRate, target) {
    var monthlyRate = annualRate / 12;
    var balance = principal;
    var month = 0;

    // Repeat while the balance of the investment is less than the target.
    while (balance < target) {
        var interest = Math.round(balance * monthlyRate * 100) / 100;
        balance += interest;
        month++;
    }
    return month;
}
</script>
</head>
```

principal	annualRate	interest	balance	month

target	monthlyRate

m

```
<body>
<button type="button" onclick="testInvest()">Test</button>
<div id="outputDiv"></div>
</body>
</html>
```

Greatest Common Divisor

The greatest common divisor (**gcd**) of two non-zero integers is the largest positive integer that divides both numbers without a remainder. An efficient algorithm to compute the gcd was discovered by Euclid and works like this. Given two integers, 102 and 18,

1. divide 102 by 18 to get a quotient of 5 and a remainder of 12,
2. divide 18 by 12 to get a quotient of 1 and a remainder of 6,
3. divide 12 by 6 to get a quotient of 2 and a remainder of 0
4. the remainder 0 means the greatest common divisor of 102 and 18 is 6.

Euclid's algorithm is written on the next page inside a JavaScript function that has this header: function gcd(a, b). Notice from its header that the gcd function requires two values as parameters. To call this function a programmer must write the name of the function, gcd, followed by an argument list with two arguments to match the two parameters, as shown in the testGCD function below.

Example 16
```
<!DOCTYPE HTML>
<html lang="en-us">
<head>
<meta charset="utf-8">
<title>Greatest Common Divisor</title>

<script type="text/javascript">
/* Input: No user input
 * Processing: Determine the greatest common divisor of -24 and 472
 * Output: The greatest common divisor
 */
function testGCD() {
    var x = -24;
    var y = 472;
    var divisor = gcd(x, y);
    document.getElementById('outputDiv').innerHTML = divisor;
}
```

Desk Check

x	y	divisor

```
// Finds and returns the greatest common
// divisor of two integers a and b.
function gcd(a, b) {
    // Ensure a and b are not negative.
    a = Math.abs(a);
    b = Math.abs(b);

    // Ensure a is greater than or equal to b.
    if (a < b) {
        var swap = a;
        a = b;
        b = swap;
    }

    // Loop until the greatest
    // common divisor is found.
    do {
        var r = a % b;
        a = b;
        b = r;
    } while (b != 0);

    return a;
}
</script>
</head>

<body>
<button type="button" onclick="testGCD()">Test</button>
<div id="outputDiv"></div>
</body>
</html>
```

r	a	b	swap

Common Mistakes

Putting a space in a function's name

Incorrect
```
function check Answer() {
}
```

Correct
```
function checkAnswer() {
}
```

Forgetting the opening or closing curly brace

Incorrect
```
function sum(x, y, z) {
    var s = x + y + z;
    return s;
```

Correct
```
function sum(x, y, z) {
    var s = x + y + z;
    return s;
}
```

Re-declaring or re-assigning parameters

```
function getDiscountRate(birthday, gpa) {
    // Wrong! Don't re-declare nor assign parameters.
    var birthday = new Date("3/17/1995");
    var gpa = window.prompt("What is your GPA?");

    var birthYear = birthday.getFullYear();
    var currYear = new Date().getFullYear();
    var age = currYear - birthYear;
    var rate;
    ...
    return rate;
}
```

Confusing the concepts of return and output

Return means to return a value to the call point of a function. This is entirely internal to a program, and the user will not see anything because of a return statement. To return a result from a JavaScript function, use the keyword return.

Output means to show a value to the user. In JavaScript output is done by calling window.alert, document.write, or assigning a value to the innerHTML attribute of a div (document.getElementById('resultDiv').innerHTML = x;).

Chapter Summary

- A function is a reusable part of a program that performs one task such as calculating the average of a list of numbers or the area of a triangle.
- A function has a header, also called the signature, and a body.
- The header of a function includes the function's parameters. Each parameter is a variable. The values for a function's parameters come from the point in the program where a function is called.
- The body of a function includes all the statements to perform a task such as a calculation and a return statement to return a calculated value to the call point.
- To call a function, write the function's name followed by the arguments that the function will need to perform its task.
- To store the value returned from a function write a variable name and the assignment operator (=) at the call point of the function.

Review Questions

1. Write the header for a function named coneVolume which takes as parameters a radius and a height.

2. Write the header for a function named computeFutureValue which takes as parameters three numbers named principal, annualRate, and years.

3. Write code to call a function that has this header:

   ```
   function addOrder(name, amount)
   ```

4. Write code to call a function that has the following header. Also, assign the result returned from the function to a variable named p

   ```
   function isPrime(value)
   ```

Programming Assignments

1. Rewrite the number guessing game code found in review question 10 of chapter 8 so that it
   a. is inside a function with this header: `function numberGuessGame()` which is called when a user clicks a Play button
   b. chooses a different pseudo random number between 1 and 100 each time it runs
   c. counts the number of guesses the user takes to correctly guess the answer

2. Create an HTML document which contains a text field, a button, and a div. The first text field should be labeled "Fahrenheit" and the button should have the text "Celsius" written on it. Write two functions with these headers:

```
function doInputOutput()
function fahrToCels(fahr)
```

   The first function (`doInputOutput`) must be called from the `onclick` attribute of the button and must do the following:

   a. get a temperature in Fahrenheit from the text field
   b. call the second function (`fahrToCels`)
   c. store the value returned by `fahrToCels` in a variable
   d. output the value returned by `fahrToCels` to the div for the user to see

   The second function (`fahrToCels`) must

   a. take a temperature in Fahrenheit as a parameter
   b. calculate the corresponding Celsius temperature
   c. return the Celsius temperature

   In other words, the second function (`fahrToCels`) must not gather any input from a user and must not output anything for a user to see. Instead it must calculate and return the result which makes this second function very reusable in other projects.

3. Create an HTML document which contains two text fields, a button, and a div. The first text field should be labeled "Temperature", and the second should be labeled "Wind Speed". The button should have the text "Wind Chill" written on it. Write two functions with these headers:

```
function doInputOutput()
function windChill(tempF, speed)
```

The first function (doInputOutput) must be called from the onclick attribute of the button and must do the following:
   a. get a temperature from the first text field
   b. get a wind speed from the second text field
   c. call the second function (windChill)
   d. store the value returned by windChill in a variable
   e. output the value returned by windChill to the div for the user to see

The second function (windChill) must
   a. take a temperature in Fahrenheit as a parameter
   b. take a wind speed in miles per hour as a parameter
   c. calculate the wind chill factor as a temperature in Fahrenheit
   d. return the wind chill factor in Fahrenheit

In other words, the second function (windChill) must not gather any input from a user and must not output anything for a user to see. Instead it must calculate and return the result which makes this second function very reusable in other projects.

The formula for computing the wind chill factor is

$$f = 35.74 + 0.6215\,t - 35.75\,s^{0.16} + 0.4275\,t\,s^{0.16}$$

where f is the wind chill factor in Fahrenheit, t is the air temperature in Fahrenheit, and s is the wind speed in miles per hour at five feet above the ground. Use your function in an HTML and JavaScript program that includes two text fields to input the air temperature and wind speed and a div to output the wind chill factor.

4. Create an HTML document that looks similar to Figure 33. Write two functions with these headers:

```
function doFV()
function computeFutureValue(principal, annualRate, years,periodsPerYear)
```

The first function (doFV)
   a. takes no parameters
   b. is called from the onclick attribute
   c. gets input from the user
   d. calls the computeFutureValue function
   e. displays the result to the user

The second function (computeFutureValue) computes and returns the future value of an investment. The formula for computing the future value of an investment is $f = a(1 + r)^n$ where f is the future value, a is the investment amount, r is the growth rate **per period**, and n is the **total number of periods** throughout the life of the investment.

Figure 33: The user interface for an investment calculator.

5. Create an HTML document that looks similar to Figure 34. Write four functions with these headers:

```
function doPayment()
function doBalance()
function computePayment(principal, annualRate, years, periodsPerYear)
function computeBalance(principal, annualRate, years, periodsPerYear,
        numberOfPaymentsPaidToDate)
```

The first two functions (doPayment and doBalance)
a. take no parameters
b. are called from an onclick attribute
c. get input from the user
d. call the computePayment or the computeBalance function
e. display a result to the user

The computePayment function computes and returns the monthly payment for a loan with a fixed annual interest rate. The formula for computing a loan payment is

$$p = \frac{ar}{1 - (1 + r)^{-n}}$$

Figure 34: The user interface for a loan calculator.

where p is the payment per period, a is the loan amount, r is the interest rate **per period**, and n is the **total number of periods** throughout the life of the loan.

The computeBalance function computes and returns the balance for a loan with a fixed annual interest rate. The formula for computing the balance of a loan after n payments have been made is

$$b = a(1 + r)^n - \frac{p((1 + r)^n - 1)}{r}$$

where b is the balance, a is the loan amount, r is the interest rate **per period**, p is the payment per period, and n is the **number of payments paid to date**.

Chapter 10. Arrays

An **array** is a collection of variables where each variable has the same data type, for example, an array of integers or an array of Student objects. Each variable in an array is called an **element** and has an **index**, also called the **subscript**, which denotes that element's location within the array. One advantage of using arrays is that all the elements within an array can be declared, created, or passed to a function as a whole. However, each element may still be accessed individually by using the element's index. Figure 35 shows a representation of an array with 10 elements. Notice that each element has a unique index, and in JavaScript indexes are always non-negative integers with 0 as the first index.

Figure 35: A representation of an array showing the elements and indexes.

Chapter Outcomes

By the end of this chapter you will be able to:

- Declare, create, and populate an array.
- Write code to access a single value within an array.
- Write a loop to process every element in an array.
- Write code to sort and search an array.
- Use the methods in the Array object to process arrays.

Declaring an Array

Just like a variable must be declared before it can be used in a program, an array must also be declared. To declare an array in JavaScript, a programmer writes the keyword var followed by the array's name, exactly the same as declaring a variable.

Template

```
var arrayName;
```

Example 1

```
var data;
var scores;
```

Creating an Array

Declaring an array in JavaScript does not cause the computer to reserve space for the elements of the array. To do this, a programmer must also create the array. All objects, including arrays, are created in JavaScript using the keyword new.

Template

```
arrayName = new Array(size);
```

Example 2

```
data = new Array(6);
scores = new Array(25);
```

In the previous example, the first line causes the computer to reserve space for an array that holds 6 values with indexes numbered from 0 to 5 inclusive. The second line causes the computer to reserve space for an array named scores that holds 25 values numbered from 0 to 24 inclusive.

It is possible to combine the array declaration and creation into a single statement.

Example 3

```
var data = new Array(6);
var scores = new Array(25);
```

Example 4

Declare and create an array named altitudes that has 50 elements in it.

It is also possible to declare, create, and initialize the elements in an array in a single JavaScript statement.

Template

```
var arrayName = [ value0, value1, … valueN ];
```

Example 5

```
var measures = [ 4.7, -3, 2.1, 0, 7.2 ];
```

Handbook for Beginning Programmers

Example 6

Declare and create an array named degrees that has these numbers inside it: 25.2, 18.0, 31.6, 22.1

Array Length

All arrays in JavaScript automatically have an attribute named length which is the number of elements contained in the array.

Template

```
arrayName.length
```

Example 7

```
var data = new Array(8);
var sizes = [ 4.7, 5.8, 2.1, 3.9, 7.2 ];
document.getElementById('div1').innerHTML = data.length;    // displays 8
document.getElementById('div2').innerHTML = sizes.length;   // displays 5
```

Accessing an Element

To access a single element within an array either to read or write the element's value, simply write the name of the array followed by the index of the element in brackets. In JavaScript, an index is always a non-negative integer, and the very first index is always 0. An index is never a fractional number because it doesn't make sense to ask what is stored in an array at a fractional index, for example 3.8. There is a value stored at index 3 and a value stored at index 4 but nothing stored at index 3.8.

Template

```
arrayName[index]
```

Example 8

```
var data = new Array(6);
data[0] = 1.3;
data[1] = parseFloat(document.getElementById('input1').value);
⋮
document.getElementById('output').innerHTML = data[4];
⋮
if (data[5] > 6.3) {
    document.getElementById('error').innerHTML =
            'Data value is too high!';
}
```

Example 9

Write a statement to store the number 72.6 in an array named ranges at location 3.

Filling an Array

It is often desirable to have the computer initialize all the elements in an array to some value (usually zero). We do this by writing a statement that assigns a value to one element in the array, and then put that assignment statement inside a loop. If the array has n elements in it, then the loop causes the computer to repeat the assignment statement n times, once for each element in the array.

Example 10 contains a function that fills an array with some value x. Of course, in order for the code in the function to be executed, a programmer must write code to call the function similar to this code:

```
var list = new Array(80);
fill(list, 7);
```

which creates an array with 80 elements and calls the fill function to store the number 7 in each element of the array.

Example 10

```
// Fills the specified array with the value x.
function fill(list, x) {
   // For each index in the array named list
   for (var i = 0; i < list.length; i++) {
      // store the value in x in the array
      list[i] = x;
   }
}
```

Desk Check

list

| [0] | [1] | [2] | [3] |

x: 8.3   i

Handbook for Beginning Programmers

Filling an Array with a Ramp

Within programs that perform image processing, we often use an array as a **palette** or **look up table**. To get the color value of a pixel, the computer reads the value of the pixel stored in the image and then looks up that value in the palette. Then the computer displays the color from the palette at the corresponding pixel location on the monitor. Often the palette must be initialized to contain values that are constantly increasing, for example: 0, 1, 2, 3... This is known as a ramp because if you plotted the values in the array, you would see a sloping line or ramp, constantly increasing to the right as shown in Figure 36.

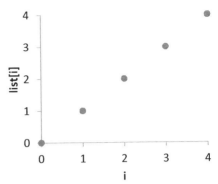

Figure 36: A plot of constantly increasing values forming a ramp.

Here is a code example showing how to initialize an array to an increasing ramp.

Example 11

```
// Fills the specified array with constantly increasing
// values from 0 to list.length - 1, inclusive.
function ramp(list) {
    for (var i = 0;  i < list.length;  i++) {
        list[i] = i;
    }
}
```

Desk Check

list   i

[0] [1] [2] [3] [4]

Occasionally we want to initialize an array to hold constantly decreasing values such as: 15, 14, 13 ... 0. This is known as a reverse ramp because if you plotted the values in the array, you would see a sloping line or ramp, constantly decreasing to the right as shown in figure 15. Example code to initialize an array to a reverse ramp is shown below.

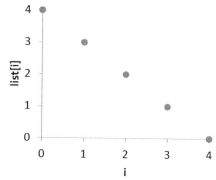

Figure 37: A plot of constantly decreasing values forming a reverse ramp.

Example 12

```
// Fills the specified array with constantly decreasing
// values from list.length - 1 to 0, inclusive.
function reverseRamp(list) {
    var high = list.length - 1;
    for (var i = 0;  i < list.length;  i++) {
        list[i] = high - i;
    }
}
```

Desk Check

list   high   i

[0] [1] [2] [3] [4]

Reversing an Array

Reversing the order of the elements in an array is not commonly used in computer programs. However, it is an interesting operation and understanding it helps students to understand more commonly used array operations. One way to reverse the elements in an array is to use two index variables, one index starts at the beginning of the array, and the other starts at the end of the array. Then write a loop that repeats $n / 2$ times where n is the number of elements in the array. Each time through the loop, the computer switches one element in the left half of the array with one element in the right half.

Example 13

```
// Reverses the contents of the specified array.
function reverse(list) {
    var left = 0;
    var right = list.length -1;

    while (left < right) {
        // Exchange two elements.
        var swap = list[left];
        list[left] = list[right];
        list[right] = swap;

        // Move the indexes toward the center.
        left++;
        right--;
    }
}
```

Desk Check

list

3.4	−2	5	7	12
[0]	[1]	[2]	[3]	[4]

left	right	swap

Summing the Values in an Array

Within a program, we often have a series of numbers stored in an array, and the program needs to calculate the sum of those numbers. This is easily done by writing a function with a variable to hold the sum and a loop that adds each value in an array to that variable.

Example 14

```
// Returns the sum of the values stored in an array.
function sum(list) {
    var s = 0;
    for (var i = 0; i < list.length; i++) {
        s += list[i];
    }
    return s;
}
```

Desk Check

list

3.4	-2	5	7	12
[0]	[1]	[2]	[3]	[4]

i	s

Finding a Value (Linear Search)

Very often a computer program must determine if a certain value is stored in an array or not and if stored in the array, then return the value's location. The value to be found is called the *key*. If the array is not too large (perhaps less than 100 elements), finding the key can be easily done using a linear search. A linear search is done by comparing each element in the array with the key until the key is found in the array or the end of the array is reached.

The advantage of a linear search is that it is simple and easy to code. The disadvantage is that it is too slow if the array has many elements in it. When the array has many elements in it, it is probably faster to sort the array and keep it sorted and to use a binary search to find the key within the array.

JavaScript code to perform a linear search is shown below. In the example, if the key is found in the array, the search function returns the index of the location within the array where the key was found. If the key is not found, the search function returns −1.

Example 15

```
// If key is in list, returns the first index where
// key is located within list; otherwise returns -1.
function linearSearch(list, key) {
    for (var i = 0;  i < list.length;  i++) {
        if (list[i] == key) {
            return i;
        }
    }
    return -1;
}
```

Desk Check

list

28.1	20	23.6	0	15
[0]	[1]	[2]	[3]	[4]

key	i	return
23.6		

Handbook for Beginning Programmers

Finding a Range

Sometimes a computer program has a list of numerical ranges and must find the range that contains some value. Examples of this type of computing problem include:

- determining a person's income tax rate from a list of income ranges and graduated tax rates
- determining a customer's discount rate from a list of purchase ranges and discount rates
- determining a salesperson's commission from a list of sales ranges and commission rates
- determining a student's letter grade from a list of score ranges and letter grades

For example, a company may offer discounts to its customers where the discount rate is based on the amount purchased according to this table.

If the purchase amount is greater than or equal to	And the purchase amount is less than	Then the discount rate is
0	$300	0%
$300	$600	2.0%
$600	$1000	2.5%
$1000	∞	3.0%

A beginning programmer will often code a JavaScript solution to this problem like this:

Example 16

```
// Computes and returns a discounted purchase amount.
function getDiscountedAmount(purchase) {
    var rate = 0;
    if (purchase >= 0 && purchase < 300) {
        rate = 0;
    }
    if (purchase >= 300 && purchase < 600) {
        rate = 0.02;
    }
    if (purchase >= 600 && purchase < 1000) {
        rate = 0.025;
    }
    if (purchase >= 1000) {
        rate = 0.03;
    }
    var discount = purchase * rate;
    return purchase - discount;
}
```

Desk Check

purchase	rate	discount	return
$708.00			

After a little practice, the beginning programmer realizes that the separate `if` statements can be connected with `else` and that the `else` part of each `if` statement will be executed only when the previous `if` part is false. This means the code can be written more succinctly and achieve exactly the same results by removing the left half of each `if` statement.

Example 14

```
// Computes and returns a discounted purchase amount.
function getDiscountedAmount(purchase) {
    var rate;
    if (purchase < 300) {
        rate = 0;
    }
    else if (purchase < 600) {
        rate = 0.02;
    }
    else if (purchase < 1000) {
        rate = 0.025;
    }
    else {
        rate = 0.03;
    }
    var discount = purchase * rate;
    return purchase - discount;
}
```

Desk Check

purchase	rate	discount	return
$708.00			

The problem with both these solutions is that if the company changes the purchase amount ranges or the discount rates, then a programmer must change the corresponding code. An improved solution is to remove the ranges and rates from the code and place them in a file or database so that the computer can read them into an array when it runs the program. Then the programmer must write a simple linear search method to find the correct range and the corresponding discount rate as shown in the next example.

Example 18

```
// The values in these arrays can be hard coded
// into your program, or even better, they can
// be read from a file or a database.
var limits = [ 300, 600, 1000 ];
var rates = [ 0, 0.02, 0.025, 0.03 ];

// Computes and returns a discounted purchase amount.
function getDiscountedAmount(purchase) {

    // Find the purchase range.
    for (var i = 0;  i < limits.length;  i++) {
        if (purchase < limits[i]) {
            break;
        }
    }

    // Get the discount rate that
    // corresponds to the purchase range.
    var rate = rates[i];

    //
    var discount = purchase * rate;
    return purchase - discount;
}
```

Desk Check

limits

300	600	1000
[0]	[1]	[2]

rates

0	0.02	0.025	0.03
[0]	[1]	[2]	[3]

purchase	i	rate	discount	return
$708.00				

Finding a Value (Binary Search)

If the elements in an array are sorted, then the computer can use a faster algorithm called **binary search** to find an element within that array. The binary search algorithm works by comparing the key to the middle most element in the array. If the key is greater than the middle most element, then the search is repeated in the last half of the array. If the key is less than the middle most element, then the search is repeated in the first half of the array. Of course, if the key is equal to the middle most element, then the key has been found and the search is done. This process of comparing the key to the middle most element of the current interval is repeated until the key is found or the interval has shrunk to only 1 element. If that one element is not the same as the key, then the key is not present in the array, and the function below returns a negative value.

Example 19

```
// If key is in list, returns any index where key is
// located within list; otherwise returns -insertPoint - 1.
// Assumes list is already sorted.
function binarySearch(list, key) {
    var left = 0;
    var right = list.length - 1;
    while (left <= right) {
        var mid = left + ((right - left) >>> 1);
        var cmp = key - list[mid];
        if (cmp > 0) {
            left = mid + 1;
        } else if (cmp < 0) {
            right = mid - 1;
        } else {
            return mid;
        }
    }

    // key is not present in list, but if it
    // were, it would be stored at location left.
    return -(left + 1);
}
```

Desk Check

list

−2.1	−1	3.9	6.2	7.1	9.7	10	12	13.1	15.6	18	19	20.1	24.5
[0]	[1]	[2]	[3]	[4]	[5]	[6]	[7]	[8]	[9]	[10]	[11]	[12]	[13]

key	left	right	mid	cmp	return
15.6					

If the key is not present in the array, the return value of the binary search function above is -insertPoint - 1. In other words, if the key is not present in the array, the index where key should be inserted can be found using this code:

```
var index = binarySearch(list, key);
if (index < 0) {
    var insertPoint = -index - 1;
}
```

In the binarySearch code above, the statement that computes *mid* needs some explanation. Here is the line:

```
mid = left + ((right - left) >>> 1);
```

The right shift operator (>>>) shifts all the bits in an integer to the right which is the same as using integer division to divide a *non-negative* integer by a power of two. However, the right shift operator executes faster than division. To help us understand the statement, we can rewrite it by replacing >>> 1 with / 2.

```
mid = left + Math.floor((right - left) / 2);
```

Notice that this statement uses the Math.floor function to truncate (not round) the result of the division. Also notice that if this were an algebraic expression, it could be simplified to

```
mid = Math.floor((left + right) / 2);
```

which is easier to understand. From this simplified formula we see that the midpoint is simply the left index plus the right index divided in half. However, because of number overflow, if we use the simplified formula in the code, it may not work for very large arrays, and so we must use the more complex formula.

Array Methods

JavaScript includes several useful methods that you can use to manipulate the contents of arrays.

Array Methods

Method	Description
a.concat(item1, item2, …)	Returns a new array composed of the original array and the argument arrays or values.
a.every(func, thisArg)	Returns true if a test function returns true for every element in an array.
a.filter(func, thisArg)	Returns a new array that contains all elements that passed a test function.
a.forEach(func, thisArg)	Calls a function once for each element in an array.
a.indexOf(toFind, start)	Returns the index within the array a of the first occurrence of the element toFind, or -1 if not found.
a.join(separator)	Joins all elements of an array into a string.
a.lastIndexOf(toFind, start)	Returns the index within the array a of the last occurrence of the element toFind, or -1 if not found.
a.map(func, thisArg)	Returns a new array that contains the results of calling a function on every element in an array.
a.pop()	Removes and returns the last element from an array.
a.push(item1, item2, …)	Adds one or more elements to the end of an array.
a.reduce(func, thisArg)	Returns an accumulated value produced by calling a function on every element in an array.
a.reverse()	Reverses the elements in an array.
a.shift()	Removes and returns the first element from an array.
a.slice(start, end)	Returns a new array that is a copy of elements between [start, end).
a.some(func, thisArg)	Returns true if a test function returns true for at least one element in an array.
a.sort(compareFunc)	Sorts the elements of an array in place.
a.toString()	Returns a string representing an array.
a.splice(start, count, item1, item2, …)	Removes and adds elements to an array.
a.unshift(item1, item2, …)	Adds one or more elements to the beginning of an array.

Handbook for Beginning Programmers

Sorting an Array

The best way to sort an array is to use the sort functionality provided by the programming language you are using because this built in sorting functionality has been optimized and tested. JavaScript includes built in sort functionality which is in the Array object. Shown below is JavaScript code to sort an array using the built in functionality.

Example 20

```
var vegetables = [ "Radish", "Carrot", "Tomato", "Pea" ];
vegetables.sort();
```

If you wish to sort elements in a different order than the one provided by the JavaScript language, then you must write a comparison function and pass that function as a parameter to the sort function. This next JavaScript example shows how to sort text strings in descending order.

Example 21

```
/* Compares two values, s1 and s2 and returns -1
 * if s1 should come before s2, 1 if s1 should come
 * after s2, and 0 if the two values are equal. */
function descend(s1, s2) {
    if (s1 > s2)
        return -1;
    if (s1 < s2)
        return 1;
    return 0;
}

var vegetables = [ "Radish", "Carrot", "Tomato", "Pea" ];
vegetables.sort(descend);
```

By default the built in sort function in JavaScript sorts arrays lexicographically which essentially means alphabetically. This causes problems if you wish to sort an array of numbers.

Example 22

```
var numbers = [ 7, 10, 8, 16, 3, 35 ];

// WARNING: this will sort the numbers array
// alphabetically and not numerically.
numbers.sort();
```

In the previous code, after the computer calls the sort function, the values in the numbers array will be [10, 16, 3, 35, 7, 8]. By default the built in JavaScript sort function places 10 and 16 before 3, 7, and 8 because 10 and 16 begin with 1 and alphabetically 1 comes before 3, 7, and 8. To force JavaScript to sort an array according to its numeric values, we have to pass a comparison function into the sort function.

Example 23

```
<!DOCTYPE HTML>
<html lang="en-us">
<head>
<meta charset="utf-8">
<title>Compound Interest</title>

<script type="text/javascript">
/* Input: No user input
 * Processing: Test the built-in JavaScript sort function
 * Output: The contents of an array before it is
 *      sorted, and the contents after it is sorted.
 */
function testSort() {
    var numbers = [ 7, 10, 8, 16, 3, 35 ];
    document.getElementById('output').innerHTML = numbers + '<br>';
    numbers.sort(compareNumbers);
    document.getElementById('output').innerHTML += numbers;
}

/* Compares two numbers by subtracting the second from the
 * first which will return a negative number if the first
 * number should be placed before the second, a zero if the
 * two numbers are equal, and a positive number if the first
 * number should be placed after the second. */
function compareNumbers(x, y) {
    return x - y;
}
</script>
</head>

<body>
<button type="button" onclick="testSort()">Sort an Array</button>
<div id="output"></div>
</body>
</html>
```

Handbook for Beginning Programmers

You might be wondering how a sort function works. There are many different, well known sort algorithms (selection, exchange, insertion, heap, quick, etc.). They all work by repeatedly comparing elements in an array to other elements in the array and simply moving the elements around within the array. Shown below is JavaScript code to sort an array using the insertion sort algorithm. Insertion sort is a simple and reasonably fast algorithm, although it is usually not as fast as the quick sort algorithm.

Example 24

```
// Sorts the contents of the specified array in
// ascending order using the insertion sort algorithm.
function sort(list) {
    var first = 0;
    var last = list.length - 1;
    for (var i = last - 1;  i >= first;  i--) {
        var swap = list[i];
        for (var j = i + 1;  j <= last;  j++) {
            if (swap <= list[j]) {
                break;
            }
            list[j - 1] = list[j];
        }
        list[j - 1] = swap;
    }
}
```

Desk Check

list

| 6 | -8 | 9 | 7 | 0 |
| 6 | -8 | 9 | | |

| 6 | -8 | | | |

| 6 | | 0 | 7 | 9 |

| | | | 7 | 9 |
[0] [1] [2] [3] [4]

first last i swap j

Common Mistakes

Forgetting that the first index in a JavaScript array is always 0

Incorrect

```
for (var i = 1;  i < a.length;  i++) {
    a[i] = 0;
}
```

Correct

```
for (var i = 0;  i < a.length;  i++) {
    a[i] = 0;
}
```

Going beyond the end of an array

Incorrect

```
for (var i = 0;  i <= a.length;  i++) {
    a[i] = 0;
}
```

Correct

```
for (var i = 0;  i < a.length;  i++) {
    a[i] = 0;
}
```

Chapter Summary

- An array is a collection of variables. Each variable in an array is called an element and has a unique index which denotes that element's location within the array

- To declare an array, use the keyword var.

- To create an array which will reserve space in main memory for the elements of the array, write code that uses the keywords new and Array, like this template:

  arrayName = new Array(*size*);

- To create and populate an array with known values write code that uses square brackets ([and]) like this template:

  arrayName = [value0, value1, ... valueN];

- All arrays in JavaScript automatically have an attribute named length which is the number of elements contained in the array.

- To access a single element within an array either to read or write the element's value, use bracket notation:

  arrayName[*index*]

- To process all the elements in an array, a programmer will usually write a loop that counts from zero to the length of the array similar to this:

  ```
  for (var i = 0;  i < array.length;  i++) {
      // Process each element of array using i as the index.
  }
  ```

- JavaScript includes many built-in methods that process arrays, including: concat, indexOf, lastIndexOf, pop, push, reverse, and sort.

Review Questions

1. Write JavaScript code to declare and create an array named data that has 75 elements.

2. Write JavaScript code to call the fill function as given in example 10 of this chapter and pass the array created in the previous question to the fill function.

3. Write JavaScript code to declare and create an array named samples that holds these values: 72, -3, 59, 0, 16.

4. Write code to output (display to the user) the value stored at index 1 in the samples array.

Programming Assignments

1. Write a function that creates and returns an array that contains the values: 1908, 5, 10. The function must have this header:

    ```
    function mothersDay()
    ```

2. Write a function that returns the sum of the first and last values in an array. The function must have this header:

    ```
    function addEnds(list)
    ```

3. Write a function named getMiddle that returns the value of the middle element in an array. If the array has an even number of elements, then this function must return the average of the two middle elements. The function must have this header:

    ```
    function getMiddle(list)
    ```

4. Write a function named countEvens that counts and returns the number of even integers in an array. The function must have this header:

    ```
    function countEvens(list)
    ```

5. Write a function to multiply each element in an array by some value. The function must have this header:

    ```
    function multiply(list, multiplier)
    ```

    For example, if the multiply function were called like this:

    ```
    var list = [ 17, 8, 9, 5, 20 ];
    var products = multiply(list, 3);
    ```

    The multiply function would return an array with thcse values: [51, 24, 27, 15, 60]

6. Write a function to rotate the elements in an array to the right. In other words, the function must move each element from its location to the location immediately to the right, and then move the last value from its location to the first location (not necessarily in that order). The function must have this header:

    ```
    function rotateRight(list)
    ```

Handbook for Beginning Programmers

7. Write an HTML document with two text areas and a button. Write a JavaScript program that will
   a. read all the text from the first text area,
   b. split the text into lines of text in an array,
   c. sort the array, and
   d. display the sorted lines in the second text area.

8. Write an HTML document with two text areas and a button. Write a JavaScript program that will
   a. read all the text from the first text area,
   b. split the text into numbers in an array,
   c. sort the array, and
   d. display the sorted numbers in the second text area.

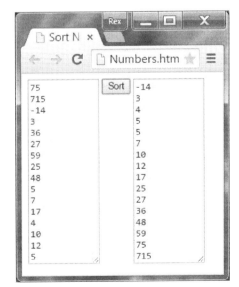

9. Write a JavaScript program that allows a user to enter a list of names in a text area. When the user clicks a button the program should output the list of names without any duplicated names. In other words the program should output each name once only. Hint: The program should read the names from the left text area and store them in an array. Then it should sort the array, remove the duplicate names from the array, and display the names in the right text area.

10. Here is an array that holds a representation of all the cards in a deck Rook cards.

```
var cards = [
    "Green 1", "Green 2", "Green 3", "Green 4", "Green 5",
    "Green 6", "Green 7", "Green 8", "Green 9", "Green 10",
    "Green 11", "Green 12", "Green 13", "Green 14",
    "Yellow 1", "Yellow 2", "Yellow 3", "Yellow 4", "Yellow 5",
    "Yellow 6", "Yellow 7", "Yellow 8", "Yellow 9", "Yellow 10",
    "Yellow 11", "Yellow 12", "Yellow 13", "Yellow 14",
    "Black 1", "Black 2", "Black 3", "Black 4", "Black 5",
    "Black 6", "Black 7", "Black 8", "Black 9", "Black 10",
    "Black 11", "Black 12", "Black 13", "Black 14",
    "Red 1", "Red 2", "Red 3", "Red 4", "Red 5",
    "Red 6", "Red 7", "Red 8", "Red 9", "Red 10",
    "Red 11", "Red 12", "Red 13", "Red 14", "Rook Bird"
];
```

Read about the Fisher-Yates shuffle algorithm at wikipedia.org. Then write a JavaScript program that will shuffle the strings in the cards array and display the shuffled cards in a text area.

11. Write a function that uses an array and no if statements to solve the Arabic number to Roman numerals programming assignment as given in chapter 6.

Chapter 11. Objects

When a programmer writes a large program, it is difficult for the programmer to keep all the code organized. One way to keep the code in a large program organized is to use object oriented programming. **Object oriented programming** is a way of viewing the world and designing and implementing software that matches the world.

Chapter Outcomes

By the end of this chapter you will:

- Understand the terms object and class
- Understand object-oriented relationships aggregation, composition, inheritance, dependency, and association
- Understand multiplicities applied to aggregation, composition, and association
- Read a UML class diagram
- Create a JavaScript object from a built-in prototype object
- Access an attribute from a JavaScript object
- Call a function from a JavaScript object

An **object** is anything in the world that has these four things:

Identity	A unique name or identification number
Data	These are characteristics of an object and are usually adjectives. These are also called attributes, properties, characteristics, fields, instance variables, or structure.
Behavior	These are the things an object does and are usually verbs. These are also called functions, operations, methods, or procedures.
Relationships	These are links or connections between objects.

A **class** is both a group of similar objects and a pattern for creating objects. Since an object has identity, data, behavior, and relationships and since a class is a pattern for creating objects, then a class must have those four things as well.

The Unified Modeling Language

Many programmers use diagrams to design and document the classes and objects in their programs. The most common language used for these diagrams is the **Unified Modeling Language** (UML). One type of diagram in the UML is the **class diagram**. Figure 38 shows a UML class diagram with two classes. Within a class diagram, each class is shown as a rectangle usually with three sections. The first section contains the name of the class. The second section contains a list of the data that all objects created from the class will have. The third section contains a list of the behaviors that all objects created from the class will have.

Student
-firstName
-lastName
-address
-phone
+changeName()
+register()
+attendClass()
+withdraw()

Course
-number
-title
-description
-location
+open()
+allowStudent()
+close()

Figure 38: A UML class diagram showing two classes.

Relationships

There are several different relationships that can exist between objects or classes. Relationships between classes are shown as different types of lines connected to the classes.

Aggregation   A relationship between two objects such that one object contains the other object. This is sometimes called a whole-part relationship. In order to use aggregation between two objects *whole* and *part*, one of these English phrases must make sense: *whole* contains *part* or *whole* has a *part*. The UML symbol for aggregation is a solid line with an unfilled diamond connected to the containing class:

Composition   A relationship between two objects such that one object contains the other object and the contained object may not be shared. This is also a whole-part relationship and is a strong form of aggregation. In order to use composition between two objects *whole* and *part*, one of these English phrases must make sense: *whole* contains *part* or *whole* has a *part*. The UML symbol for aggregation is a solid line with a filled diamond connected to the containing class:

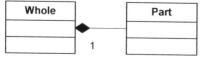

Inheritance
A relationship between two classes that causes the child class to automatically have everything (data, behavior, and relationships) that the parent class has. In order to use inheritance between two objects *parent* and *child*, one of these English phrases must make sense: *child* is a kind of *parent* or *child* is a *parent*. The UML symbol for inheritance is a solid line with an unfilled triangle connected to the parent class.

Dependency
A relationship between two objects such that one object requires or uses the other object to accomplish a task. In order to use dependency between two objects x and y, one of these English phrases must make sense: x uses y or x requires y or x needs y. The UML symbol for dependency is a dashed line with an open arrow head connected to the required or needed class.

Association
A general relationship between objects. When two objects are related but the relationship is not aggregation, composition, inheritance, or dependency, then use association. The UML symbol for association is a solid line.

11. Objects

Multiplicities

Multiplicities are small numbers and punctuation at one or both ends of a relationship that constrain the relationship. A single number multiplicity constrains a relationship to exactly that number of objects. Two or more numbers separated by commas constrain a relationship to exactly one of those numbers of objects. Two numbers separated by two periods (..) constrain a relationship to a range of objects. For example, multiplicities may be used to show that one egg carton has either 12 or 18 eggs inside it as shown in Figure 39.

Figure 39: A UML class diagram showing two classes with multiplicities.

Multiplicity Examples

Multiplicity	Meaning
1	Exactly one
4,8	Exactly four or exactly eight
0,1	Zero or one, also known as optional
0..1	Zero or one, also known as optional
12..18	Between 12 and 18 inclusive
0..*	Zero or more
*	Zero or more
1..*	One or more, also known as at least one
3..*	Three or more, also known as at least three

Handbook for Beginning Programmers

Example 1

Label the parts of this UML class diagram, including class, attributes, operations, aggregation, composition, inheritance, association, and multiplicities.

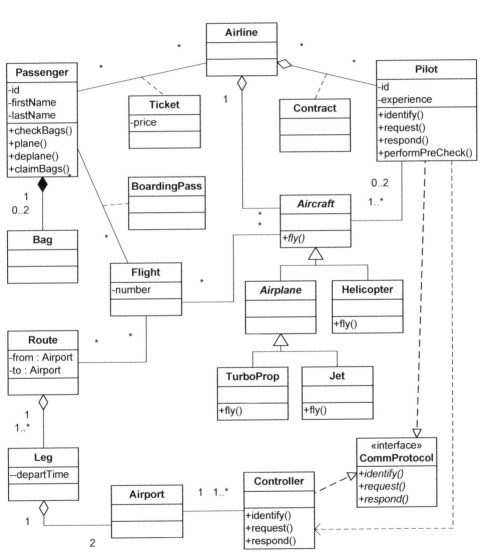

Figure 40: A UML class diagram for an airline.

Example 2

The following diagram shows many of the elements of the JavaScript programming language and the relationships among those elements. The relationships are shown using UML symbols.

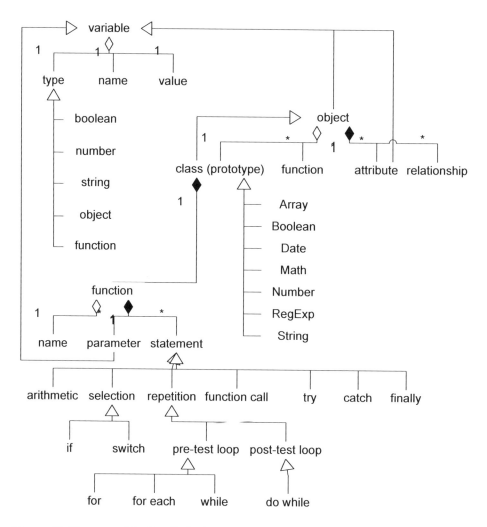

Figure 41: Elements of the JavaScript language and the relationships among those elements.

JavaScript Built-in Objects

Following is a list of the JavaScript prototype objects that a programmer can use to create new objects and a list of other JavaScript objects that a programmer can use in a program.

JavaScript Prototype Objects

Object Name	Purpose
Array	Stores multiple values as a single variable
Boolean	Stores either true or false
Date	Stores a date and time
Number	Stores a numeric value
String	Stores text
RegExp	Used to match patterns in text

Other JavaScript Objects

Object Name	Purpose
Math	Contains constants and functions used in calculations
window	An open window in a browser where an HTML document is displayed to the user
document	The HTML document that is open in a window

Declaring an Object

Just like a variable must be declared before it can be used in a program, an object must also be declared. To declare an object in JavaScript, a programmer writes the keyword var followed by the object's name, exactly the same as declaring a variable.

Template

```
var objName, objName2, … objNameN;
```

Example 3

```
var now;
var s;
```

Creating an Object

Declaring an object in JavaScript does not cause the computer to reserve space in memory for the attributes of the object. To do this, a programmer must also create the object. All objects are created in JavaScript using the keyword new. In many programming languages a programmer must write the name of a class after the new keyword. However, JavaScript doesn't have classes, but instead has prototype objects. So after writing the new keyword, a JavaScript programmer must write a prototype object's name.

Template

```
objectName = new PrototypeName(arg1, arg2, … argN);
```

Example 4

```
now = new Date();
s = new String();
```

In the previous example, the first line of code causes the computer to create a Date object that will hold the date and time of the moment that it is created in the computer's memory. The second line causes the computer to create an empty String object. It is possible to combine an object declaration and creation into a single statement.

Example 5

```
var now = new Date();
var date = new Date('2015/04/25');
var s = new String();
var n = new Number(103.7);
```

It is also possible to declare, create, and initialize an object in a single JavaScript statement.

Template

```
var objectName = { attrib1Name : value1, attrib2Name : value2 … };
```

Example 6

```
var student = {firstName:'Samuel', address:'125 W Main', height:1.78};
```

student : Object
firstName = 'Samuel'
address = '125 W Main'
height = 1.78

Figure 42: A UML object diagram showing one object.

Handbook for Beginning Programmers

Accessing an Attribute

To access an attribute of an object either to write or read the attribute's value, simply write the name of the object followed by a period (.) followed by the name of the attribute.

Template

```
objectName.attributeName
```

Example 7

```
// Store 'Jill' in a student object's firstName attribute.
student.firstName = 'Jill';

// Read the firstName attribute from a student object.
var f = student.firstName;
```

Calling a Method

A **method** is a function that is part of an object. To call a method, simply write the name of the object, a period (.), the name of the function, and an argument list.

Template

```
objectName.funcName(arg1, arg2, … argN);
```

Example 8

```
date.setFullYear(2025);
var s = date.toDateString();
```

Chapter Summary

- Object oriented programming is a way of viewing the world and designing and implementing software that matches the world.
- An object is anything in the world that has identity, data, behavior, and relationships to other objects.
- A class is both a group of similar objects and a pattern for creating objects.
- The Unified Modeling Language (UML) is a diagramming language that lets a software developer draw classes and objects.
- JavaScript includes several prototype objects including Array, Boolean, Date, Number, String, and RegExp, that a programmer can use to create new objects.

- To create a JavaScript object use the new keyword and the name of the prototype object:

  var *objectName* = new *PrototypeName*( );

- To read or write the value of an object's attribute, use the name of the object and the name of the attribute separated by a period:

  objectName.*attributeName*

- To call a function that is part of an object, use the object's name and the function's name separated by a period:

  objectName.*funcName*(arg1, arg2, …);

Review Questions

1. Write JavaScript code to declare and create a Number object named fifty that holds the value 50.

2. Write JavaScript code to declare and create a Date object named overflow that holds the date January 19, 2038.

3. Write JavaScript code to display the value of PI from the Math object.

4. Write JavaScript code to call the sqrt function in the Math object to compute the square root of 75.

Chapter 12. Strings

Within a computer program the term **string** refers to a string of text or a group of characters strung together. When writing JavaScript code, a good way to visualize a string is as an array of individual characters inside an object with 0 as the index of the first character.

Chapter Outcomes

By the end of this chapter you will be able to:

- Create strings that include special characters as escape sequences.
- Use the length attribute of a string.
- Access a single character within a string.
- Compare two strings.
- Use the built-in string methods.

Creating a String

To create a string you can use a string literal inside single (') or double (") quotes or the new keyword.

Templates

```
var name = 'any text here';
var name = "any text here";
var name = new String(thing);
```

where *thing* is any valid JavaScript expression to be converted to a string.

Example 1

```
var title = 'Oh Say, What is Truth?';
var other = "Truth Reflects upon Our Senses";
var another = new String('Put Your Shoulder to the Wheel');
```

Example 2

```
var x = 3;
var s = new String(x);
```

String Concatenation

To create a large string of text from smaller strings of text you can use the **string concatenation** operator which is the plus symbol (+). For example:

Example 3

```
var name = "Samantha";
var message = "Hello, " + name + ". How are you today?";
```

Escape Sequences

Occasionally you will want to include single or double quotes or other special characters in a string literal. You can include a special character by placing a backslash character (\) immediately before it. Within a string literal a backslash followed by one or more characters is called an **escape sequence**. You can also write escape sequences to include Unicode characters (see unicode.org/charts) in a string literal that you would not be able to type from your keyboard. This includes mathematical symbols and characters from languages other than English.

JavaScript Escape Sequences

Sequence	Description
\b	Backspace
\f	Form feed
\n	New line
\r	Carriage return
\t	Horizontal tab
\v	Vertical tab
\0	Null character
\'	Single quote
\"	Double quote
\\	Backslash
\udddd	The Unicode character specified by the four hexadecimal digits dddd. For example the copyright symbol (©) is \u00a9.

Example 4

```
var quote = "Mr. Churchill declared, \"Never give in!\"";
var greek = 'The first three letters of the Greek alphabet are \u03b1 \u03b2 \u03b3';
```

Within a string literal, the backslash at the end of a line causes the string literal to continue on to the next line.

Example 5

```
var intersect = 'The mathematical symbol for \
intersection is an upside down U like this: \u2229';
```

String Length

Just like arrays, all strings in JavaScript automatically have an attribute named `length` which is the number of characters contained in the string.

Template

```
name.length
```

Example 6

```
var title = 'Carry On';
document.getElementById('output').innerHTML = title.length; // displays 8
```

Accessing a Character

Just like an array you can use the bracket operators ([and]) to retrieve a single character from a string. Also just like an array, the index of the very first character in a string is 0.

Template

```
var varName = strName[index];
```

Example 7

```
var title = 'Carry On';
var c = title[4];  // the variable c will hold 'y'
```

Because a JavaScript string is an array inside an object each string has several methods that you can call. The `charAt` method does the same thing as the bracket operators: retrieve the character at a given location.

Example 8

```
var title = 'Carry On';
var c = title.charAt(4);  // the variable c will hold 'y'
```

Comparing Strings

To compare strings in JavaScript, you can use the relational operators (<, >, <=, >=, ==, and !=) just as you would for numbers.

Example 9

```
var output;
var a = 'always';
var b = 'believe';
var c = 'always';

if (a < b) {
    output = a + ' is less than ' + b + '. ';
}
else {
    output = a + ' is equal or greater than ' + b + '. ';
}

if (a == c) {
    output += a + ' equals ' + c;
}
else {
    output += a + ' does not equal ' + c;
}

document.getElementById('outputDiv').innerHTML = output;
```

Desk Check

a	b	c	output	
'always'	'believe'	'always'		

Handbook for Beginning Programmers

String Methods

JavaScript includes several useful string methods that you can use to manipulate the contents of strings.

String Methods

Method	Description
s.charAt(index)	Returns the character at the given index.
s.charCodeAt(index)	Returns a number indicating the Unicode value of the character at the given index.
s.concat(s2[, s3, ..., sN])	Combines the text of two or more strings and returns a new string.
s.contains(toFind[, start])	Returns true if the string s contains the characters of the string toFind.
s.endsWith(toFind[, start])	Returns true if the string s ends with the characters of the string toFind.
s.indexOf(toFind[, start])	Returns the index within the string s of the first occurrence of the string toFind, or -1 if not found.
s.lastIndexOf(toFind[, start])	Returns the index within the string s of the last occurrence of the string toFind, or -1 if not found.
s.replace(toFind, replacement)	Used to find a match between a regular expression and a string, and to replace the matched substring with a new substring.
s.split([sep][, limit])	Splits a string into an array of strings by separating the string into substrings.
s.startsWith(toFind[, start])	Returns true if the string s starts with the characters of the string toFind.
s.substr(start[, length])	Returns the characters of a string starting at the specified index and continuing for the specified number of characters.
s.substring(start[, end])	Returns the characters of a string between two indexes into the string.
s.toLowerCase()	Returns a copy of the string s with all characters converted to lower case.
s.toUpperCase()	Returns a copy of the string s with all characters converted to upper case.
s.trim()	Trims whitespace from the beginning and end of the string.

Reversing a String

Occasionally you will want to reverse the order of the characters in a string. This is easily done with a loop and string concatenation.

Example 10

```
// Reverses the contents of a string.
function reverse(s) {
    var rev = '';
    for (var i = s.length - 1;  i >= 0;  i--) {
        rev += s.charAt(i);
    }
    return rev;
}
```

Desk Check

s	i	rev
'pool'		

Extracting a Substring

Many computer programs store people's names in this format: *FamilyName, GivenName* (a person's family name followed by a comma and a space followed by the person's given name). When names are stored in this format, a common operation is to extract the family name as done in this function.

Example 11

```
// Extracts a person's family name from his full name.
// This function assumes fullName contains a string in
// this format:  FamilyName, GivenName
function extractFamilyName(fullName) {
    var comma = fullName.indexOf(', ');
    var family = fullName.substring(0, comma);
    return family;
}
```

Desk Check

fullName	comma	family
'Washington, George'		

Handbook for Beginning Programmers

Counting Characters

Another common operation with strings is to count how many times a specific character occurs in a string. This can be done with a loop and an if statement.

Example 12

```
// Returns the number of times that the
// character stored in c occurs in the string s.
function countOccurrences(s, c) {
    var count = 0;
    for (var i = 0;  i < s.length;  i++) {
        if (s.charAt(i) == c) {
            count++;
        }
    }
    return count;
}
```

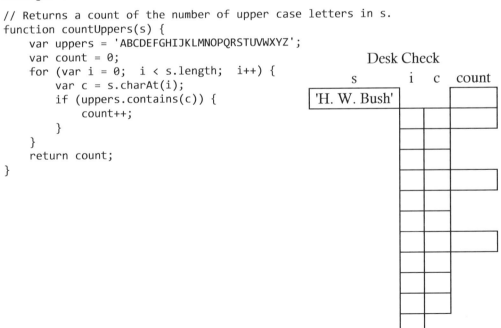

You may also want to know how many upper case letters are in a string which can be done very similarly to the previous example.

Example 13

```
// Returns a count of the number of upper case letters in s.
function countUppers(s) {
    var uppers = 'ABCDEFGHIJKLMNOPQRSTUVWXYZ';
    var count = 0;
    for (var i = 0;  i < s.length;  i++) {
        var c = s.charAt(i);
        if (uppers.contains(c)) {
            count++;
        }
    }
    return count;
}
```

Chapter Summary

- To create a string surround text with single or double quotes.
- To include special characters, such as single quote ('), double quote ("), or new line, in a string use an escape sequence: \' \" \n etc.
- To read or write a single character within a string, use the bracket operators [and] like an array: *stringName*[*index*];
- To compare to strings, use the comparison operators: ==, !=, <, <=, >, and >=
- JavaScript contains many useful built-in string methods.

Review Questions

1. Write JavaScript code to declare a string named address and assign the text "123 W Main" to it.

2. What character is at index 4 in the string literal in the previous question?

3. Write JavaScript code to retrieve the character at index 4 from the variable address and to store that character in a variable named c.

4. Write JavaScript code to convert all the characters in a string named s to lower case and assign the lower case string to a variable named t.

Programming Assignments

1. Write a function named extractGivenName with one parameter named fullName. The parameter fullName will always contain a person's family and given names in that order separated by a comma and a single space, for example "Reagan, Ronald" (without the quotation marks). The function should extract and return the person's given name, for example "Ronald" (without the quotation marks).

2. Write a function named prefix that returns the common prefix of two strings. For example, the common prefix of "disable" and "distasteful" is "dis". This function takes two parameters and returns the common prefix.

3. Write a function named suffix that returns the common suffix of two strings. For example, the common suffix of "swimming" and "walking" is "ing". This function takes two parameters and returns the common suffix.

4. Write a function named switchCase that receives a parameter named s. This function must return a new string that contains the same characters as s but with the case of every character switched. For example if switchCase were called like this: switchCase("Catch 22"); it would return "cATCH 22" (without the quotes).

5. Write a function named titleCase with one parameter named s. This function returns a copy of s but with the first letter of each word capitalized.

Appendix A. Operator Precedence

Operator precedence determines the order in which the computer evaluates operators. Operators with higher precedence are evaluated first. For example $7 + 3 * 2$ is 13 because multiplication has a higher precedence than addition, so the computer performs the multiplication before the addition.

Associativity

Operator associativity determines the order in which the computer evaluates operators of the same precedence. There are two categories of associativity, left to right and right to left. Consider the expression: a OP1 b OP2 c

Left to Right Associativity

If OP_1 and OP_2 have the same precedence and left associativity (left to right) then the computer will evaluate the expression as: (a OP_1 b) OP_2 c
For example, the computer evaluates $3 - 5 + 4$ as $(3 - 5) + 4$ which is 2.

Right to Left Associativity

If OP_1 and OP_2 have the same precedence and right associativity (right to left) then the computer will evaluate the expression as : a OP_1 (b OP_2 c)
For example, the computer evaluates a = b = 5 as a = (b = 5) by first storing 5 in b, then storing the value of b in a.

Precedence

Listed from highest precedence (evaluated first) to lowest precedence

Operator(s)	Name(s)	Associativity
( )	parentheses	n/a
. [ ]	member	left to right
++ --	increment, decrement	n/a
+ - ! ~	unary plus, negation, logical not, bitwise not	right to left
* / %	multiplication, division, modulus	left to right
+ -	addition, subtraction	left to right
<< >> >>>	bitwise shift	left to right
< > <= >=	relational	left to right
== !=	equality	left to right
&	bitwise and	left to right
^	bitwise exclusive or (xor)	left to right
|	bitwise or	left to right
&&	logical and	left to right
||	logical or	left to right
? :	conditional	right to left
= += -= *= /= %= <<= >>= >>>= &= ^= |=	assignment operators	right to left
,	comma	left to right

Appendix B. Robust Code

There is an old computer programming joke that goes like this. A consultant went to a large company to teach the software engineers in the company. At the beginning of the class she said to the students, "If you got on an airplane and realized that your team had written the software that runs the airplane, how many of you would be afraid for your life and get off the plane?" Every student except one put his hand up. The consultant looked at the one student who didn't raise his hand and asked, "What does your team do differently so that you wouldn't be afraid to ride on the airplane?"

The student answered, "Ha! If my team had written the software, the plane would never even get off the ground. I'd be perfectly safe."

Below are some programming practices that if you follow will make your software more robust (fewer errors) and help you rest easy on a working airplane for which you and your team wrote the software.

1. Turn on compiler warnings and never ignore them.
2. Follow generally accepted coding standards and conventions, including naming conventions.
3. Write and use assertions. Test primarily with assertions turned on.
4. Write and execute unit tests and don't ignore test failures.
5. Whenever possible, write simple, straight forward code. For example when writing in JavaScript, Java, C++, and C do not use the left shift operator (<<) to multiply by a power of two. Instead use multiplication (*) and rely on the compiler to generate fast code.
6. Write each function to perform one and only one task.
7. Minimize the number of execution paths through your code. (See the section Finding a Range in chapter 10 of this book for an example of how to do this.)
8. Write each function with only one exit point (return statement).
9. Consider writing a tricky algorithm twice, once with a straight forward, slow solution and once with a sophisticated, fast solution. In the debugging version of your program use the slow solution to verify the results of the fast solution.
10. When writing in a language that has exceptions, never return error codes from a function. Instead throw exceptions to indicate an error.

Index

-- (decrement), 53
– (negation), 46
' (single quote), 32, 175
– (subtraction), 46
! (logical not), 81
!= (not equal), 63
" (double quotes), 32, 175
% (modulus), 46
&& (logical and), 81
( ) (parentheses), 47
* (multiplication), 46
/ (division), 46
/* (multi-line JavaScript comment), 31
// (single line JavaScript comment), 31
[ ]. *See* array index
\ (backslash). *See* escape sequence
^ (logical exclusive or), 81
|| (logical inclusive or), 81
+ (addition), 46
+ (string concatenation). See string
   concatenation
++ (increment), 53
< (less than), 63
<!-- (HTML comment), 18
<= (less than or equal), 63
= (assignment), 46
== (equal to), 63
> (greater than), 63
>= (greater than or equal), 63
aggregation, 166
algorithm, 12
And, 81
array, 143
   element, 143
   index, 143, 145
   length, 145
   subscript. See array index
Array object, 156, 171

ASCII, 7
association, 167
attribute, 165, 173
bit, 5
boolean, 42
break, 106
byte, 5
case, 69
class, 165
composition, 166
concatenation. See string concatenation
control structure, 15
Date object, 171, 172
De Morgan's laws, 86, 91
defining table, 11
dependency, 167
desk check, ix, 45
do while, 98, 101
else, 65
escape sequence, 176
exclusive or, 81
flow of execution, 15
for, 99, 101
for each, 100, 101
function, 42, 121, 126
   argument, 127
   call point, 124, 127
   header, 121, 126
   parameter, 126
   return, 122, 127, 136
   signature. See function header
getElementById, 34
gigabyte, 5
gigahertz, 5
Heron's formula, 130
hertz, 5
if, 64
if else, 65

About the Author

Rex A. Barzee is a professor of Computer Information Technology at Brigham Young University – Idaho. He is an inventor of two United States patents and the author of numerous books. He earned a bachelor's and master's degree in Computer Science from Brigham Young University. Before becoming a professor he worked in industry for eight years as a software engineer for Southwest Research Institute, Hewlett-Packard Company, Voyant Technologies, and the Utah State University Space Dynamics Laboratory. He worked on a variety of projects including the HP-UX kernel, the HP-UX standard C library, HP-UX OpenGL 3D Graphics Library, full text indexing, image processing, and VoiceXML applications. You can see his full profile at LinkedIn.

Other Books by the Author

21642365R00115

Made in the USA
San Bernardino, CA
30 May 2015